AN ANGEL SPEAKS

SECOND VOLUME
IN THE SAMUEL THE PROPHET SERIES

HELEN PORTEOUS

First published in Australia by Aurora House

This edition published 2025
Copyright © Helen Porteous 2025

Typesetting and e-book design: Amit Dey (amitdey2528@gmail.com)
Cover design: Donika Mishineva (www.artofdonika.com)

ISBN number: 978-1-923298-15-6 (paperback)

A catalogue record for this book is available from the National Library of Australia

OTHER BOOKS
BY HELEN PORTEOUS:

The Samuel the Prophet series
Samuel Says

The Fairy Folk series: a Helen Porteous and Linda Lycett collaboration
Fairy Folk and Other Strange Little Creatures
Fairy Folk and the Magical Helpers
Fairy Folk and Fantastic Friends
Fairy Folk and Their Wonderful World
Old Man Dots

Writing as H. M. Porteous:

Sandy the Flipper Dragon

Acknowledgements

A book doesn't instantaneously spring into reality, fully formed and ready to be read. There is an intensive and sometimes frustrating process when the author starts putting onto paper, using one method or another from among the many, the thoughts, insights, and information they want to share with others.

And when it is timely, a team of professionals takes over and continues this creative process until a finished book is offered to the reader. From the author, editors, publishing staff, and the distributors of the book, there are many helpers along the way.

My full gratitude goes to the Upside Team, a group of Spirit Authors and Helpers who have always been with me. Their strong, ongoing encouragement has been invaluable, and instrumental in me being able to accomplish what I promised to do many years ago.

My thanks also go to all members of the wonderful and professional Aurora House publishing team, who have been so friendly and helpful across the board; and so, a very heartfelt thank you for the kindness and the patience offered to me at all stages of getting Samuel's words into print.

DEDICATION

Samuel's words are dedicated to all readers
who are interested in new ideas, unusual insights,
and the strengthening of every individual's
intuitive knowledge.

CONTENTS

INTRODUCTION

It is 7.40 on a pleasant Wednesday morning and I have before me, on the table, pens and paper all arranged neatly and ready for action. The pens have freeflowing ink, and the paper is stacked within easy reach.

Today, Samuel and I have a date, an agreed-upon day when we begin the next book in the 'Samuel' series. I am curious as to what is going to be written in this second book, because the first book we 'wrote' together, *Samuel Says*, was an interactive, fascinating, and extremely interesting experience for me, with many new ways of explaining insights and spiritual information coming to light. It was also fun and educational to work within its unusual parameters, and a delight to work with such a wise wordsmith as Samuel is proving to be.

All manuscripts in this series will be dictated by Samuel, who says he is known to some of us by the name Samuel the Prophet and recorded by me using the writing technique called automatic writing.

As the words come through, they are accompanied by a full range of images, insights, and strong emotions, including humour and earnestness, comical scenarios, love, and empowerment. What comes through at any given time really depends on what Samuel is talking about.

I hold the pen loosely in my hand with the ink making contact with the paper, I totally relax and allow my hand to move where it needs to go, and when the energy of 'Samuel' connects or slams a bow wave of energy into the room like a freight train on steroids, my hand begins moving purposely across the paper.

Words, then sentences, are formed. The words are two dimensional but come in a total package, and I feel extremely privileged to be doing this creative work with Samuel. Maybe one day a new process will enable the reader of these words to release the embedded 'extras' as their eyes pass over the print, the embedded 'extras' that Samuel says is encoded within the words, thus giving the reader a new range of deeper understanding and interaction with the messages.

Samuel introduced himself to me during an extraordinary evening many years ago. Prior to this day, in my daily meditations, I had been seeing strong visions of a man who looked as though he came from ancient times. These visions flashed by quickly and I had no idea who this image represented.

On this extraordinary night, I was attempting to do at least some legible automatic writing. This was something I had tried to do now and again over the years, but the attempts were never fully successful. My interest in metaphysics was and still is intense, and I have read and studied many different aspects of it over the years, so I knew in theory how automatic writing worked.

I had a heavy quartz pendulum with me, and I planned to use it to ask questions and bring forth the 'yes' or 'no' answers to general questions. But shortly after I began working with the pendulum, something unusual happened.

The pendulum began to dip and circle in unusual ways, and at the same time, the energy in the room changed in an exciting manner. The crystal began defying gravity, swinging up and out in all ways that seemed impossible. It literally seemed to come alive!

At the same time, the energy in the large room became electrified, and it was amazing and exhilarating to feel. The joy, the power, and the wonderful feeling of laughter permeated everything, and the pendulum continued to do its impossible dance movements. The energy was electric.

I put down the pendulum and picked up the practice pen and paper. The more I 'let go', the freer and faster the words came scrawling onto the paper, seemingly out of the blue. At the start of the writing, the answers to my questions came as a basic 'yes' or 'no', but the situation rapidly changed, and as the wonderful energy in the room intensified, so too did the legibility of the words.

The pen held loosely in my hand began to move with purpose and started to write the words that became the opening sentence of a most amazing and extraordinary essay. Not all the words were legible at the beginning, and the sentence structure was not easy to understand in places. Some words were even repeated for me, but the end result of this automatic writing session totally changed my life. The first sentence was "Spirits write essay on humanity".

Until the essay was finished, the joyful and powerful electric feeling in the room remained and even intensified, the huge windows rattled, and the room filled with dancing, sparkling lights. It was a magical time, and I could feel the 'rightness' and sheer joyfulness of it all.

The essay that came through on this pivotal night follows word for word:

"The place of work is everywhere. How do we feel about it all? What is the essence of the whole exercise? What do you want to say or learn? Do the [*unknown word*] wasteful times may be small-minded people, so that small-minded people can understand? Is this what you want to see?

"No, not a waste of time; no, not at all. It is all important so be patient. Small things make a major difference. Wellness is a state of mind, so must be allowed to develop at the most marked [*I'm not sure if this is the correct word*] place and time.

"What is the meaning of all the [*unknown word*] manner of work that has been well-written most of the time? When the Spirits call the shots. Most of the words must be wellwritten news with all that has been done, must be nitty gritty and profound at all times.

"How will the people waste moments all the while? What is the most wanted message that all will want to know? How will we tell when the message is the correct one, when your world is in the worst worries imaginable? Your day of troubles is not so far away."

At this stage I could feel a major, heavy zapping sensation all over my body. The entire room was still joyously electrified.

"Yes, it will not be so far away that the time to start learning is here. So, when we talk is near. What will be the outcome of all the books and letters that have been mustered at this time? When will the news come out into the open and shake the wowsers out of their dogma and open their eyes? When will the news be mostly needed?

"Always. Many will be gone, and all the news will mostly mean nothing to the masses at this time of mournage. How will the masses be able to cope without the news of deliverance and hope? Who will be the lucky ones, and who will be the worried ones when the sadness is at the peak of times?

"How will they be able to say they are delivered when they don't know what to say and feel about all things? What do the people believe, that they are not able to understand?

"So, what is the answer to all this? What is the final solution? It is the teaching of the news to the masses and the

HOPE of all the good things to come. The Almighty Gods are about and plentiful with the LOVE OF ALL THINGS."

That was the end of the essay, and it was signed with a flowing, looping and swirling sort of 'L' letter that looked almost like an 'S' reversed. It was at this stage I asked who was writing this, because I knew it wasn't me. The name Samuel was written and, as the ink flowed, the windows of the room rattled and shook strongly, the energy absolutely stunning. It was an extraordinary moment.

I asked if 'Samuel' was one of my spirit guides and the answer came:

"No, Samuel is a Speaker, is the Teacher and Communicator."

At this stage, I got up from the chair and walked across the room towards the rattling windows, and it felt as though I was stepping into an electric current of joy, goodwill, and celebration. I was thoroughly enjoying the experience.

Much later, when I typed up my notes, I left the wordage in the essay as it came through to me on the night, because it showed how the opening words were a bit stilted, the new connection was not instantaneously legible at the beginning, my not understanding a word or phrase making a sentence unreadable, and how rapidly the words became easier to read with sentences flowing smoothly and more coherently.

Samuel kept in contact over the next four years, and gradually I found out more about this visitor who came on that Wednesday night. Little snippets of information came through now and again in the daily writings.

I was still trying to work out who 'Samuel' was. For example, in my daily journal, my Spirit friends wrote, "You have been trying to find out who Samuel is. We say this. Samuel, in your book and in historical terms, would be classed as an Archangel, one of the seven who sit beside the Lord.

"Other names are immaterial but are there. He is a Blessed One and has the Power of Love so strong that the teachings from this Great Soul need the students to understand the connections and the emotions of the word. Samuel is a Mighty Lord of the Universe, and the power of creation is immense. We, as a group of Spirit Helpers, are greatly privileged to be doing this work with, and for, the Blessed One."

I knew from the first contact all those years ago, when I was offered the chance to co-author with Spirit entities and record their words, that the plan was to record and publish books about metaphysical insights that were specifically written for people who were beginning their spiritual quest. For those readers who had a larger smattering of metaphysical knowledge, the words and insights within the books would act as gentle reminders of the basic concepts. And Samuel would be dictating the words.

In my own personal life during this time, I was going through some intense learning experiences, and I felt as though I was being continually thrown into the deep end of a pool of never-ending insights. It was an interesting and challenging time for me, and at the back of my mind, I knew Samuel was looking over my shoulder, encouraging me, pushing me, and loving me.

The first book was eventually published, and *Samuel Says* is the title. This volume is the next book in the series. I am looking forward to working with Samuel again as this book, *An Angel Speaks*, comes into existence.

PREFACE

Dictated by Samuel

G ood day to you, dearest readers, it is a pleasure being with you again. To the readers who are new to my words, allow me to give you a brief introduction of who it is that speaks with you.

I am an everyman, a Spirit of world note. I am in your bible as Samuel, Samuel the Prophet. I have been called by many names, but in this time frame of mankind's history, it seems appropriate to keep the 'prophet' part. You need all the prophetic help you can get to be able to survive and evolve as an enlightened species.

To the people who read the holy books, read the *Book of Samuel* again. I 'spoke' for the Creator. I received messages from God. This has not changed because in the biblical times, I was a judge of the people and a judge of their actions. Who judges people today? Who brings forth God's judgement into the lands? Who judges the judges?

Strong humour is coming through in these sentences. This feeling is quite tangible, because it is not wishy-washy or nebulous in any way. It is as though someone is having a fun time right beside you and the vibration of their laughter is going right through you. Samuel has suggested that I put in any comments I wish to make as we go along with the recording.

This is a critical time for mankind, and the Spirit World is gathering *en masse* to do what can be done to bring help and advice into the lives of one and all. I am one only, one of a multitude of angelic helpers who are connecting with you at this time of your most dire troubles.

Like the seasons that come and go, so too do the helpers and guides come and go from the Realm of Spirit. It is time again to bring forth and strengthen the love, the hope, and the blessings into the hearts of the multitudes.

You will hear of many voices bringing you these messages of the Creator. You will read of many miracles occurring in out-of-the-way places. You will listen to voices of reason being spoken by 'channelling' prophets. You will be inundated with the hope of all the good things to come.

And for the readers who do not believe in spirit messages, prophets, seers, and the like, don't fuss about the origins of these words. Read the words and judge them by what sense or non-sense they make for you. The message is the important issue, not so much the bringer of the message.

Would you like to know about the destiny of mankind?

Now, a point here ... I will call the human race 'mankind', not 'men and women', or 'something else', kind. In this day of nit-picking and political rules and regulations, I realise that I will be seen to be politically incorrect with my wordings. God the Creator, is God, both male, female, it, and everything in between. And I write the word in whatever way it wants to come forth at the time of writing.

My bluntness may offend some readers, especially those whose sensibilities are too finely tuned to hear the truth put clearly before them. I will not apologise for the way I speak, but in return, I will send love and understanding into the hearts of the easily offended ones. Life is not meant to be bound by rigid, narrow boundaries of what can and cannot be spoken in someone's presence, just in case the words are deemed too blunt.

Look into the heart of the messages and the ideas expressed in the book. If I can make you think about an issue or a core belief in a new way, or show you another angle to see events from, then I will be a happy prophet indeed.

The words are being written with the help of my dearest daughter Ahale. I call everyone daughter or son, so do not jump to erroneous conclusions. Anyway, in the big Universal Scheme, you would find it difficult to prove this is an erroneous name calling.

Again, good humour twists and floats with the words and gleefully flows onto the page. It is such an uplifting and good feeling to have at any time around yourself, let alone at the start of what may be an emotional time as we work through the manuscript. The words and emotions seem to slam into my brain with their clarity. And my hand struggles to move fast enough across the paper when the intensity is high. It is difficult to describe easily what is fully going on during the dictation, because there are so many things happening at the same time.

You will have read Ahale's brief description of our initial meeting, and the awareness and congenial state of this writing partnership. This will have shown you that there is infinite patience and planning going on at all times to bring the communication between our worlds, our different realities, close and then closer.

Therefore, dear readers, know that these books of 'Samuel' have been prepared and readied over time. Do not think that Ahale's experience is an unusual one. Indeed, there are many, many spirit contacts happening right now. Some messages will come as written ones, and some will come through in musical forms. And some will come through dreamtime adventures. They will come in all ways, all ways.

I am one of many, yet the many are me. In times of troubles we come, we come. Open your hearts to our words, because we speak with the Love of the Universe in our hearts. The most beloved angel Mary is one such Speaker and we work together yet again. This beautiful one is also an author of many words, and she has a series of already written booklets.

Many more books and literature of all sorts will be written, because it is time for mankind to take the next evolutionary step. We stand behind you, ready to help, and ready to push you into the next level of your learning.

I am Samuel.

Samuel the Prophet.

Listen well, dearest readers, listen well, and read with understanding and patience.

Blessed be.

A brief explanation here regarding the Mary comments: Samuel's first contact was many years ago, and then he went silent. From that time on, I was waiting and wondering when the book dictation by Samuel would start. Instead, years later, while I was writing in my daily journal, the word "essene" came through on the top line of a new page.

I didn't do anything about the word and continued to write down the everyday contact information. The word was repeated and repeated until I suddenly realised that the atmosphere in the room had changed. I asked who was writing the word and the answer came back "Mary".

This was the beginning of a beautiful experience, and it was a true privilege to work with her. From the beginning of this working relation-ship, I was told there would be twelve small books written and they would be written in a simple manner, so that those who were beginning the search for their spiritual path would understand the simple analogies of what can be, in fact, complex and difficult to understand insights.

The twelve books were finished on a Mother's Day. I felt that it was an appropriate day to finish her series on.

1

THE UNIVERSAL GIFT STORE — THE PRESENTS AND THE PRESENT

It is now 8.a.m. A good morning, dearest daughter. Are you ready to begin?

I start by speaking of everyday things, describing them with everyday words, but they are words and situations that will have immense concepts within their meaning.

The way of the prophet is to bring to attention the possibilities and probabilities of what is to be. Think carefully on this opening sentence. You should immediately note that I have not said 'what will be', because nothing in existence is set in stone, and all existence is alive and dancing with changeable energy.

Your past is still in the flux of change; your present and your future are also in the throes of this volatile and enriching energetic change. Do you believe I am telling you a larcenous lie with these words? Do you feel that so-called past history is over and done with, and all that is left of these old events are the records in dusty history books? Do you believe these older events have stopped influencing world opinions and world consciousness?

The so-called past is alive and well, and is influencing you in many, many ways as you go about your daily life. Influencing you even as you sit reading this book.

Think carefully on the next statement. As you walk around the kitchen, as you move around your office or your place of work, doing whatever you are doing, your thoughts, feelings, and energetic projections are influencing and changing your past, the present, and your future.

At this point, please do not say, "Oh dear, this prophet is a little old-fashioned, because he does not seem to understand what is happening in the modern-day world."

In answer to this, I say to you that I come from a long line of souls, who have been interacting with mankind down through the ages. I tell you this: there is nothing, nothing that is set in motion that does not flow outwards and inwards, forward and backwards, upwards and downwards, affecting everything that exists. And of course, you set in motion all your thoughts, ideas, and emotions into this energy mix.

You are all familiar with the analogy of the ever-expanding ripples that begin when a stone is tossed into a body of water. What you may not consciously remember is that this rippling energy does not stop when it reaches the furthest bank. It continues to ripple out over the land, into the earth, into the atmosphere, and everywhere in between. There is no stop sign anywhere that says:

RIPPLES MUST STOP AT THIS LINE.

And note well, it is not just the physical directions that these ripples flow through, but the dimensions that you know as 'time' and 'space', and other dimensions not yet known to mankind.

Wonderful and talented things are these ripples. Therefore, is it not logical that the energy you expend on a daily basis affects everything around you in all ways, in all time zones, and in all epochs of history?

Let me put it squarely to you. It is how you react today that determines how the 'past' is altered. So, as you can now note, a prophet is in the position to bring to your notice, possibilities and probabilities, but not set in stone any dogmatic and inflexible predictions.

The Standard English Desk Dictionary states:

PROPHET. Inspired teacher, revealer or interpreter of God's will, spokesman, and advocate: one who foretells events, e.g. Prophetic writers of the Old Testament.

Yes, this is so, but events can be foretold as long as the probability factor that leads to these predicted events remains high. In other words, predictions are predictions, and because these predictions are being stated, written, or recorded somewhere, this already puts a certain degree of solidity towards the outcome, because the words and their meanings are being manifested into the physical reality.

As an example of what I state above, the ancient prophets predicted the rise and fall of civilisations, of certain types of warfare, of aviation and flying machines that would change the way mankind lives, and so on. Many of these recorded prophetic visions have eventuated, maybe not exactly as stated, but close enough for modern scholars to call them hits.

The pattern of the Creator's Universe is one of birth, death, and rebirth. Birth, death, and rebirth: this cycle applies to everything, and I mean everything, including the weeds in your garden, the rocks in the ground, and the countless star systems in existence.

The timing between the cycles of birth, death, and rebirth is different in the various life forms that create our galaxies. Therefore, the difference is only in the timing, that is all, because the rise and fall of any civilisation is already in its gestalt, or matrix, from its onset.

Prophets are visionaries, clairvoyants, and seers who connect with this patterning and are able to see the potentiality of what is to come. They see or sense the grand plan and have the ability to open a certain limited communication with the grand master, the master planner in whatever energy nexus He, She, or It chooses to be seen as. Therefore, a prophet has certain guidelines that have already been set out, guidelines that act as a target on which to focus their attention, and so they are able to spot any variables as they begin forming.

Variables, yes indeed. If you totally believed some of the prophetic claims that have been made, the world as you knew it would have ceased to exist some time ago, and yet here you all are, still spinning around on your beautiful blue and green planet. Your world has not ended, and the Armageddon is still a vague threat for the future to deal with. Right?

Hopefully, in the Introduction you would have read the initial essay that was dictated many years ago. Since that day, your planet has seen much warfare, and it has been shaken to its core by the bombing of and tampering with the surface layers. There has been untold human misery and distress, and in general terms, a gloomy time has been had by many people in many countries.

The words that I spoke in the Introduction were common-sense words, more so than prophetic words. Yet I suggest you read this essay carefully again, especially the last few sentences. Despite all the woes and troubles for mankind, there is HOPE for all the good things to come. The Gods indeed are plentiful and willing to help bring about this Love of All Things.

The rise and possible fall of this current civilisation does not have to be as the doom and gloom predictions foretell. Indeed, the word fall is not one I would willingly use at all. I would prefer to use the word 'ascension', because I see a civilisation changing, adapting, and evolving into new and higher levels of enlightenment.

And the actual imagery of the word 'fall' suggests a downwards spiralling, a spiralling down to a baseness of behaviour and lack of understanding. Again, in the word imagery world, a fall from grace implies getting out of favour, or getting out of the Creator's good books.

Ascension also means an alteration of status. That is true enough, but the implication here is one of a rising above the baseness, the hopelessness, the despair and failing ideals. The imagery generally used is one of going 'up' to Heaven and 'down' to Hell. If you feel the human race has lost the plot and that *en masse* you have all become lost in chaos, then you are also implying a 'falling from the Creator's Grace' and this is a downwards slippery slope that has no easy return; it may become difficult or impossible to navigate out of the depths.

Now, dear readers, this I ask of you; never ever think this is so, and do not ever, ever imply or infer in any way that this is the case. If you do feel that humanity has lost the plot so to speak, you are adding your very substantial energy to the negative balance, in other words, the slippery slope, and you will be putting your considerable and influential energy at the end of the seesaw that has the sign painted with the words:

NO HOPE.

And what is also true, as more and more doom-and-gloom media stories spin emotionally downwards scenarios and you do nothing to stop this rot, then you show to all that you intrinsically agree with what is being presented to the masses. This brings more power and strength to the negative end of the teeter-totter, or in other words, the slippery slope.

If you feel that, as a member of a sentient species, the collective of humankind is in dire trouble and woe, then you are all in dire trouble and woe. What you personally, and with others, collectively create with actions, thoughts, and feelings will come into manifestation in one way or another.

At the other end of the teeter-totter is a sign painted with the word:

HOPE.

You now can understand how you become a vital factor in whatever happens in the times and places you live in. It is a numbers game after all.

There is a cheeky sense of humour tumbling through with the words.

The seesaw is balancing on its pivot, wobbling from one side to the other, and it is the changeable mass of energy that is being attracted to one end or the other that causes this wobble. A seesaw is a balance tool, and it has two opposing ends. Everything has a dual or balanced identity, for example:

Ying – Yang
Black – White
Light – Dark
Day – Night
Hope – Hopelessness
Love – Fear
Happiness – Sadness

You may readily come up with your own list, because there are unlimited dual systems for you to choose from. The precariously balanced fate of humankind is in flux right now, and it is time to choose what end of the seesaw you will put your energy towards. It is time for you to do something other than sit on the sidelines and let everybody else do the work, because there is no option available for you to be able to sit in the middle and watch both sides; therefore, this is not a viable option for you to look for.

Not only is this fence-sitting an unenlightened action in accordance with the 'cosmic rules', but you are also doing yourself a great disservice if you do not use your multitude of talents and choose to plunk yourself down firmly on the end of the teeter-totter that says HOPE.

Hey, there will be no big, stern angel who will swoop down and smite you senseless if you try to sit in the middle, or on the proverbial fence. But you must admit, it will be a sad waste of your beautiful strengths and abilities. So, sit on the fence if you must, but hear this again from me.

You don't have a great deal of time to work out where you personally want to go, what you personally want to do, and what you personally think is the best road for mankind to travel at this time. Do not forget that the seesaw is already unstable.

Let wind, rain, sunshine, and rainbows – in fact, all the elements – come and go in their cyclic ways, but it is your future, your past, and your present that needs to be thought about deeply and intuitively.

What does the word 'present' actually mean to you?

Maybe, it can mean being in the place in question or physically being ready and waiting. A gift. Being ready with assistance. Right now. To take part in. Introduce someone or something. Exhibit, to show or offer, suggest as a gift, to give as a gift.

Present.

In my words, I will put my thoughts thusly:

You are being offered a gift right now, in this specific time and place.

I offer you help, and all needed assistance to take part in what is happening now in this specific time and place.

At this interesting time, you are taking part in a magnificent creational endeavour, which is your physical manifestation on this Earth. Treat this time, this place and opportunity as a gift, a present, and as an inspiration for you to explore your present, as a gift of the **now**.

That is all for the day, dearest daughter. Be a happy person today, because all is well in your world.

It is now 8 a.m. on Easter Friday. A gentle rain is falling on a most appreciative land. As I write, a wallaby comes hopping cautiously over the rocks and passes close to the window where I am sitting. Its fur is wet and splattered, but I am sure that this gentle creature will find joy and pleasure at the present gift of the rain, because the hillside on which it lives has been very dry in the last few months, and there has been a severe shortage of food for all the native denizens.

The book dictation yesterday was of great interest to me. When a new book begins, I am in many ways exhilarated that the work has begun and an uplifting routine once again established. Yet, at the same time, I am apprehensive of what may be written. What a contradiction.

I fully believe in the validity of the words that come from my angelic friends, yet even now I am unsure at times whether I am the best person, or interpreter, to be doing this work. There are always mixed emotions, but to use Samuel's analogy of a seesaw, I feel that I am well and truly sitting on the end that says HOPE. I will put my energy towards bringing this hope, as a gift, as a present, not only into my own life but into as many other lives as I am able to.

Samuel now begins to write, with his swirling signature appearing on the page.

A present is a true gift, a gift that someone will receive and benefit from. A something that has been carefully thought through with the best interests of the receiver in mind, well before the final selection was done.

Even the small gifts exchanged between people need to be true gifts ... not just the passing forward of any unwanted or unused gifts you may have previously received on your last birthday. Or like any items you didn't like and don't feel the need to keep in the home.

These unwanted gifts, of course, may be offered to other people, given as gifts further down the chain, but each and every time, please go to the trouble of carefully selecting which present goes to whoever will be most in tune with it, or in need of this particular gift. Because in the big scheme of things, it is also the personal energy transfer from you that determines the validity and acceptance of any gift you give.

There is such a humorous atmosphere floating around and being presented with the words, and on the theatre screen behind my eyelids, there is fun imagery of gifts being shunted here and there between people until they find a true home. The imagery running on this screen is comical and informative at the same time, and it can be super hilarious if the gifts themselves get the humour of their situation.

You want to give a present that means something good or pleasant to the recipient, don't you? If you don't have an item or something physical to give, then always remember that the best gift of all is the gift of love, of friendship and caring. Your present, your gift, represents your attitude, the vibrational emanations that flow from you, as well as the physical transference of whatever it is you are giving.

The gift, the actual present itself, is a physical reminder of your ability to help others; or, if you are sitting on the other end of the seesaw where it says NO HOPE, you remind yourself of your inability to help others in any meaningful manner.

Think back on some of the gifts you have been given lately. Have you enjoyed receiving these gifts? Have these gifts been useful things that you have actually used in some way?

Maybe as a gift you were invited out for a meal, and you were taken to a beautiful restaurant where a well-cooked meal was served to you. Did you enjoy the meal and the company of the people with you? Or were you eating this meal just because you did not want to hurt the feelings of the one giving you this gift?

The choice of food on the menu may not have been appropriate for your relaxation and comfort, because the giver may not have known that you were trying to lose weight and were on a strict diet, or that you were allergic to the shellfish being offered on the menu, or whatever it was that made you reluctant to fully enjoy the beautiful food being offered.

Do you feel that the gift of a beautiful seafood meal would be a thoughtful gift, if you were unable for one reason or another, to enjoy a fish meal? Thinking things through, would you feel that the presentation to you of this meal could be classed as a good gift or not?

Of course, it is, but it was up to you to bring to the notice of the giver any of your reasons for not wanting to accept it. And please, exercise good manners and do this before you begin the journey to the place of eating, and most definitely before the order is given to the waiter.

You cannot blame the giver if the knowledge of your likes and dislikes is not there at the time of giving.

Don't take everything at face value. Look under the generosity and see the truth of the offering. For example, if the donor knew but then ignored your likes and dislikes, this is another matter. Become attuned to the reasons why you were given the gifts that you have been given.

For instance, did your friend know you are allergic to shellfish, but forgot this fact, and still booked the table in a restaurant that specialises in shellfish? Do you feel that there was genuine friendship being offered to you through this gift?

What vibes came through with the invitation? Did this invitation make you happy or did it stress you out, and leave you wondering how you would be able to get through this meal without offending your friend in any way? Indeed, the invitation may make you wonder if your friend is a true friend, or if there is some unspoken message being shown to you with this specific gift.

Of course, on the other hand, a true friend making an honest mistake about the inappropriateness of any given gift will not make you feel stressed out if you tell them of their forgetfulness. They will not be put out or embarrassed by the situation. So, do you see where I am going with this? It is the intent of the gift giver that is the important aspect of any gift giving. There is a lot of intuitive information available for you to notice even during the simplest of activities – information that will help you understand what is going on.

Right, that was an example of a small, yet significant gift of a meal, and you may wonder why I write about such mundane things in a manuscript about metaphysical concepts. But the underlying principles are the same, so we work from the simplest examples.

Think now on the bigger picture.

Hey there, I said the **bigger picture**!

What gifts are you being offered right now in the 'bigger picture' from the Universal Gift Store? Are the gifts coming with good vibrations wrapped around them? Can you even see or feel the gifts that are being offered to you? Can you see them, or are you so blinkered in everyday stress and striving that you cannot see any further than the end of your nose?

Have you set yourself up so that you limit what you receive, so whatever comes to you will only enhance your current beliefs and lifestyle choices, and you will only accept gifts that fall within these parameters? Are you afraid of getting gifts that stretch your thoughts, your imagination, and your pre-conceived boundaries about who you think you are? Do you reject the 'big picture' gifts that challenge you in any way?

Let me put it bluntly. The Universal Gift Store specialises in presents. Yes, this may be a play on words, but it is true, nonetheless. The Universal Gift Store **knows** what gift or present each person needs at the time and will deliver this present without prejudice and without limitations.

At all times you, the reader, are being presented, in your present time, with a present that you presently need.

They are gifts for you to accept, react to, understand, adapt, and co-create newness with, whether they be emotional, physical, knowledgeable, or spiritual gifts. These gifts are your current [present] learning tools, and it is up to you how these tools and situations are manipulated.

Back to the example of the diner who was given an inappropriate meal as a gift. If this person had the courage and diplomacy to explain his or her situation to the donor, there was the chance of a change of plans, a change of venue, and a change of menu. Then everyone could enjoy the gift. The given gift could then become an appropriate, fulfilling, and enriching one.

Here, there is another play on words, the 'now' in the word 'knows'. Samuel is having fun with this topic because of the multiple meanings beneath the words present/ know/ gift and so on.

The ongoing fun and good humour that plops into the words is continuous, and I feel I could repeat my comments ad infinitum and never get to explain fully the essence of the energy involved. All the while, a scenario is unfolding on the visionary screen behind my eyelids, where a wonderful time is being had by a group of friends, all enjoying a good meal.

Now, if the explanation of the gift being inappropriate was not brought out into the open at the appropriate time, and the meal so generously offered was eaten under sufferance and ill grace, no one benefited from the lovely gesture or became enriched in any way. There would have been an underlying atmosphere of stress, hostility, and tension swirling around the table, even if all the participants were polite and friendly.

Think on this for a moment; think on what the Cosmic Gift Store is gifting you with right now, in this present time. If you are not happy with, or do not agree in any way with your lifestyle and what is flowing into your life as we speak, then do you have the skills, and the diplomacy, and the patience to seek a more appropriate and more enriching influx of presents from the Universal Gift Store?

You have this personal choice available to use at all times, so how you choose to react and how you choose to accept or reject what you are being offered is your prerogative. As with the birthday meal, it is your prerogative to change what you are willing to receive, and what the ensuing results will be from any gifts and any actions you are ready to accept.

If you have followed this line of thought, it will show clearly that it is your choice to alter whatever you do not want to be experiencing, or do not want to accept into your life. All you have to do is decide not to receive the incoming vibrations in the manner they are currently being presented to you.

It is as though Samuel really knows a thing or two about the vagrancies and unexpected issues arising from gift giving, and the unintended consequences.

Be firm! Be diplomatic! Keep your thoughts set firmly on what enriches you, and enlightens you, then welcome only the appropriate gifts that arrive on your doorstep.

Now look back at our symbolic seesaw. See how it teeters and trembles while balancing precariously on the rocker? Do you now see how the peoples of the world can see and, therefore, do have their choice on which side of this balancing board they prefer, and which side has the strongest movement away from instability?

Can you now see that the Universe is presenting humankind, the collective consciousness of humankind, with constant choices, choices that will determine what happens in the future? Each and every person is responsible for making their own decisions, decisions that when combined, will determine the direction of humankind's destiny and the position reached on the evolutionary scale.

Your total life is a gift, a present that needs to be accepted with a loving heart and mind. I don't say 'soul' here, because your soul already knows that this is so, and it knows that the physical manifestation is a gift of an enriching present that you are receiving and dealing with right now.

If you don't agree with the present or presents you are receiving today, then make the decision to change them. Know well that The Universal Gift Store will hear and continue to send out presents that are asked for. At this point you need to be intuitively aware of what you truly are asking for, and what you truly believe you are entitled to.

If you do put in an order change, there will be no penalties or demerits for this action. The Store is totally impartial and will send whatever you believe in your heart that you deserve to get.

So, here is an important question you need to ask yourself. Do you truly believe that humankind deserves to become an even higher-evolving species? Or do you believe that humankind does not deserve to become an even more enlightened species?

Think carefully on your personal reasons for making this choice, because in the end, it all comes down to each person's personal choice of what they individualistically want to transpire.

Therefore, dear readers, you are faced with some rather important choices that you need to make. You have the ability to help the collective human spirit take that one step higher towards self-realisation and evolution.

This is daunting knowledge for some people to deal with, but if you think about things carefully, any choice made is not convoluted but is an easy one, because you always need to choose what makes you better, stronger in your faith in a better world, stronger in your faith of a present and a future that empowers you and everyone else. Take away the complexities of the bigger jigsaw picture and make it easier for yourself by working through smaller scenarios, instead of being overloaded by the full big picture.

Start noting carefully what is around you, then expand to what is in your world spaces. Doing it this way will bring your focus back into areas that you are more familiar with, and you will become less stressed out because of this familiarity of your personal world.

The big picture state of the world at the moment is more likely to overwhelm you if you don't feel confident with what you are doing, and if you are overwhelmed then it definitely will not be easier for you to understand and work through the choices that are being presented to you at any given moment.

And as I have already said, what is being activated in your personal world reflects as larger activities in the larger world. Now, this statement you will understand to be true on an intuitive level, but you may not consciously believe it to be true, especially when you watch the media coverage of international events.

A lot of this coverage is of the doom-and-gloom news events, and rarely about the good things that are happening. So, you may feel there is a dichotomy happening because you are happy and positive, yet the big picture events don't seem to follow these emotions.

But there are feel-good events happening side by side and intertwined with the feel-bad ones, and it is only that your global media outlets do not choose to bring both types of events to your notice, and they do this generally because of political and/or fear-based control.

From where I am, the balance between the good and the bad, the positive and the negative events is in a precarious state of balance, and this balance is at the pivotal point of our hypothetical seesaw. Yet know this fact and remember it well: the good deeds, the good vibrations, the more enlightened and aware people greatly outweigh the bad guys, and it is this mass of people that need to get up from their armchairs and plump themselves down firmly on the end of the seesaw that is labelled 'HOPE'.

The critical balance of those who hope is swinging more towards, and then into, the Light. This is such a heartening and joyful balancing of the right and not-quite-right actions. The angelic helpers are helping humanity win the battle of good intentions that is being waged against hopelessness and fear; they work from the realms they reside within and it is so heartening for these godly helpers of all persuasions, on all levels, to see this shift happening in the attitudes and actions of the people who can make such a dramatic difference to the final outcome of global populations and to feel the uplifting vibration of the journey towards HOME.

Despite what you may feel or are being told, your world is not going to hell in a hurry, nor will it self-implode because of a few greedy, grasping, misinformed, and elitist people; and by 'world', I mean your total world, physical assets, the natural earth environments, the spiritual matrix of everything, flora, fauna, the vast and unseen realms about you ... in fact, everything!

Your world is a cauldron of a spontaneous and energetic mass of bubbling and broiling chaos, and it is up to each individual to take a turn at stirring this cauldron. In my first book [*Samuel Says*] I have called this 'The Cosmic Soup'. As you stir this soup and add your ingredients of choice and presence to the mix, you alter the final outcome.

Will the soup be palatable for everyone? Will it nourish everyone or nourish only a few? Will it be cooked properly or will it be watery, burnt, or ruined in some way?

Right now, the soup is being prepared, and the baddies have thrown some unpalatable ingredients into the mix, but you alter the final outcome of the brew, because it is now your turn. You can counter the bad guys' ingredients by adding some tasty and nourishing ones of your own, if you so wish.

Ah, so you say that you cannot cook? Oh, of course you can. Follow what your heart chooses and put that into the hot pot. Then stir! You don't need to wear an apron or a tall white hat that has the word chef printed on it. There are many, many enlightened cooks in the world, and they are all doing their bit of stirring. Will you do yours?

Dearest daughter, we will stop at this point for the day.

It is now 8 a.m. on an Easter Sunday. It is gently raining. I can hear the muffled roar of the passing traffic through the trees, and a brush turkey is wandering down from the hillside, checking out the leaf litter for tasty titbits as it scritch-scratches along. It is wet and scraggly, yet it moves along with a contented air.

To continue: The present is indeed a present. Right now, right at this time, you are being given the gift of choosing your own reality. You are being encouraged by all the godly helpers around you to choose each present moment, each present gift that will bring you closer to knowing your true self. This is not an idle set of words that are put together by a bored and disinterested old spirit. I call myself a spirit because it is a short, easily remembered descriptive word of who you may think I am.

You are being presented with a golden opportunity to begin knowing who you are and what you can really accomplish when you put your total energy towards unleashing this knowledge. Who, or what do you think right now, is your true nature?

Sit for a moment and in your thoughts say clearly and succinctly who and what you believe you are. Contemplate how and why you are where you are at this moment; on how, why, and what you are meant to be doing today, tomorrow, and all the days to come.

Sit quietly, be present in the moment, and after a time note if you have come to any conclusions. Or are you having trouble articulating your answers and, indeed, are you having difficulty working out the answer at all, or even part of an answer that makes sense to you?

Now, if you find that you haven't been able to organise your thoughts clearly and logically, don't worry, because even people who totally believe or totally don't believe the 'man-written' aspect of any holy book may have unrealised religious indoctrination and wordy teachings to overcome, as well as everything else they deem may be stumbling blocks of some kind.

If indoctrinated, thoughts will flow into the habitual rut of how they have been taught to express emotions. Just because you have been taught certain things about your religion, does not make all these teachings truthful.

To make it easier to put your own thoughts into action, wipe your mind clear of any teachings you have received from outside sources. Now, I do not mean for you to forget your alphabet, your ABCs. I mean the religious teachings, or the beliefs that you may have about your God, or even your lack of acceptance that there is such a higher power or omnipotent energy.

I suggest you give yourself a blank mind screen and tell yourself that your own inner higher self will come through and show or demonstrate exactly who and what you truly are, and by association, what you are really meant to be doing on this turn of the wheel.

Can you be open minded enough to do this? Or would doing this exercise make you feel guilty that you doubt the conventional word of God, the God of your religious beliefs? The God you have been taught about by other people?

Can you be open minded enough to do this inner listening? Do you have trouble accepting there may be something that you have missed, or something that you don't understand, maybe something that you don't really want to know? Or maybe you even have misgivings about accepting some of what you have been taught by your religious teachers that may have been politically and deliberately misinterpreted? This misinterpretation may have been done by authors a great time ago, but it is still relevant text in your world today.

If you do have trouble accepting any possibility that you may have been taught mistruths, you will have a lot of hidden fear about yourself and your situation that you will need to deal with.

Why should you believe what this old spirit says? You don't have to believe a word of what I say, but this I tell you, it is up to you, and you, and you, to use your personal gifts of true discernment, of wonderful intuition, of inner knowing, to work out 'what is what', 'who is who', and 'where is where'.

It is important that you do this for yourself and not sit idly by while someone else decides your future, or what you should believe in. Or to sit idly by while someone else decides what presents are going to be offered to you, or while someone else decides whether you will accept these offered gifts or not?

This old spirit also has his axe to grind, and he has an agenda to work with, which empowers him as well as you. So do not feel that I am doing this advice-giving for gratis. I will also gain enrichment and grace from seeing you, and you, and you, yes and even you, become aware of your personal potential, and from seeing you begin to understand deeply the path you are walking along at this very moment.

I have a vested interest in humankind's ultimate survival as an enlightened and highly evolved species, because as all esoteric students will know, there are no barriers between the different vibrational levels of reality. What you do, what you emanate, ripples out and affects all vibrational levels. Full stop.

So, yes, this old angel is aware of having a personal agenda at work. It is not a political agenda or even a selfish or manipulative one. It is an agenda that flows from the heart; it flows from my heart filled with the Love of All Things, from me to you, in the hope that what is said and done will bring a true understanding of your present [now] to you. Nothing more, nothing less.

Let us stop at this point, dearest daughter. You are about to be interrupted, anyway. I bid you a very good day.

That turned out to be a short session. The energy was strong and flowing well, so I was surprised when Samuel said it was time to stop. It is enthralling to be doing this writing. The sentences come charging full bore out from the place they originate from, and this is all I will say about the origin for now, because there are many sides to this debate.

But while Samuel's words are mostly directed towards me and the pen, I see that streams of information lead off into other areas, and I know if it were possible to do so, there would be whole screeds of words written about some of the statements that are scattered here and there amongst Samuel's prose.

I see it like an ever-expanding tree of words and information rippling out into the universe. Maybe Samuel will gather some of this information back in another place, another time, another book; or maybe it is meant for the denizens of a different reality.

Am I meant to jot these ideas down somewhere and do something with them? I don't think that is what I am meant to do, but I watch and inter-react as Samuel seems to be choosing or selecting a path through a veritable maze of thoughts and ideas, with a specific destination in mind.

And despite all the other paths being inter-linked by closeness of sub-ject matter and interest, they are put aside for this time, while the end gate or the specific exit from the maze is kept firmly in mind.

The present time, the time you are living in now, has the potential to become one of the more important epochs in the total of humankind's history. You see, your history books will have given you some idea on how civilisations rise into great-ness then fall away into oblivion. This is the pattern of birth, death, and rebirth being repeated on a grander scale than your more personal scale.

Even the present idea that mankind began only a specific measurable time ago is missing wide the mark of truth. The total human history as you may know it is only one such birth–death–rebirth cycle. There have been many cycles in this patterning before your recorded times. And so, there has been a breathing in and a breathing out of civilisations much longer than scientists or archaeologists currently know about.

There is physical evidence of some of these previously unknown civilisations scattered here and there around the planet, some still hidden, and some not. At this point in the breathing cycle, there is a possibility for this pattern to change a little; because, after all, even cyclic patterns of any type do not remain exactly the same.

This change will be a vibrational one and will bring to the cycle new dimensions, the understanding of what has gone on before, the understanding of your place in the cycle that is now happening, and the understanding that this cycle is a naturally occurring movement resulting from the natural processes that have gone on before.

It is now time to break from the major path enough to allow a new element to enter the picture. A new evolutionary path or cycle is beginning. A new present for the presence of the species. It is time to shuffle the boundaries of this previous orbit so that more Light shines on all those souls who are walking this path. It is time for the Light of God, of All That Is to become as a beacon, a beacon that not just shows the path clearly, but for the Light that changes the cellular matrix of your intrinsic selves.

This Light alters personal and communal patterning in such a way that the vibrational energies become even closer and stronger to the cellular matrix. You alter the core of your being. This is the progressive step, the step that has been programmed to happen at this time in the cycle, the cycle that is within countless other cycles. Do you understand this?

It is as though a checkpoint has been reached, and a sign there says: "The people who are ready to take the next evolutionary step, come forward towards the Light. Bathe yourself in this Light and then embrace it. For those who do not want to take this evolutionary step, please take the path that leads through the door behind you and has a sign on it that says 'Stasis'."

There is a personal choice to be made, and the people who are too lazy to think for themselves do condemn themselves to an existence in an unfulfilling pattern, an unfulfilling cycle of mundaneness, until the intrinsic nature of stasis begins to break down the patterns and eventually disintegrates into disorder.

For the ones who walk forward without hesitation towards the Light, they will find themselves in a new vibrational cycle, and it is a magical cycle of enrichment and of enlightenment. After all, that is exactly what the word enlightenment means. Becoming lightened means becoming less heavy mentally, emotionally, physically, and spiritually, and becoming more in tune with the universal energy, to each other, and to everything else in between. To be lighted and enlightened is joy!

Now, for the people who have just read this and say, "What a lot of nonsense this author is talking, going on about circles and lights of different intensities of patterns and meanings", let me put your mind at ease. I talk in symbolic language. The full concept of the human species becoming a new or different species to what you are familiar with because of changes made in the DNA, the vibrational energetic levels, or changes in bodily appearance is a harder concept to both accept and readily understand.

Hence, the 'moving towards the Light' type of talk. The changes coming, and to come, will alter the basic pattern of what you perceive to be a typical human. It will not be like a physical increase in skull size or even an alteration in musculature and such. I speak of the human being becoming more a body of light and not one of physically dense muscle. I speak of the human being becoming better able to access other realms because of this change, or the lightening of the heavy physical anchor. It is indeed an extraordinary step that is looming in front of you, very daunting for some, exciting for others.

May I ask a question?

Yes, go ahead.

I have read in various metaphysical writings that mankind will put itself out of its misery by self-destruction. And there seems to be enough bull-headed war fanatics and murderous terrorists already among us capable of doing this to us all, but does this civilisation have to die or become even less than it is now, before this enlightened rebirth occurs?

There are births, deaths, and rebirths occurring all the time, big, small, and all sizes in between. The difference in timing between the cycles of a gnat and a Star system are immense, yet both these cycles overlap at one point or another.

The same happens with humanity. No, there will be no big cataclysmic event that wipes mankind [as is] from the face of the Earth. The birth, death, and rebirth cycles are going on as we speak. Each new generation has a different agenda to the generation before.

However, there are to come some mind-shattering world events that will well and truly put the panic into many complacent souls, and they will not know what to do, what questions to ask, or how to act. It will be a time of mournage for those who do not want the Light to show them the way.

Can you tell us any more about these events?

You don't need to know these for now, because knowing about them will put your focus and energy into the possibility of them occurring and so will increase their power to manifest. Focus instead on the love that abounds in everyone's heart. Focus on bringing this sometimes forgotten and unused energy out into the open. Show the unhappy ones that they do not need to be unhappy. Focus on the seesaw end that is marked HOPE.

World events will be used as triggers for action, for making good choices, and will become stimulants for waking up the sleeping populations.

As I have already said, you can alter the future if enough good people focus on the same wavelength, the same love and light. If enough of you decide to do so, you can turn tragedy into triumph; you can turn terrifying situations into extraordinary fulfilling events.

Each of you has the ability to triumph over troubles. Each of you is more powerful than you realise. All you have to do is decide that this is so. Everyone has the ability to give to themselves a truly inspiring gift or present in this, your present time.

What can I say about presents, the present, and the presence of the present? Many words, many words, but dear readers, this will be the end of this chapter for now. Oh, I was about to say 'present' instead of 'now'! I love the play on words.

Before I stop for the morning, I will say this. In my first books, I am keeping the words, the thoughts, in a basic form for easier reading. This is not in any way a put-down of the more informed readers who will understand readily the concepts and ideas expressed. I feel that there are many souls who have not yet begun to comprehend the talk in symbols, and who will not fully understand what 'walking towards the Light' really means.

My words are directed to the newcomers to these ideas. Yet even wellread readers may find some interesting ideas hidden away amongst the wordage. Not all the knowledge is put down in black squiggles; some is encoded into the patterns of the lines and letters and will need meditation or intuitive impulses to bring them forth. This will need to be done to reach the next level of knowledge that is implicit in these words. There are bits and pieces for all reading levels. I will speak more on this encoding at a later time. I bid you all a good day.

2

ANGEL WINGS AND SEARCH ENGINES — NEEDLES IN THE HAYSTACK — BLINKERS AND BLINDFOLDS

This is a different topic from the last chapter, but everything will slot nicely together before we are done with this book. Now, would you like to know more about angels in general? Are you curious enough to want to know if we have wings, halos, or golden curls? Are you curious enough to want to know what angelic happenings are going on behind the closed door, that door in your mind that seems to be often jammed in the closed position?

Would you? Would you?

Briefly, angels come in all sizes, all shapes; they are all different, and all have the ability to be true messengers of the God of Light. 'Angels' is a descriptive term. Switch the letters around and you have the word 'angles'. Angels are angles of light, movement, and vibrational energy essences. They are personality gestalts within a nucleus of this vibrating energy, and it depends on the speed or fineness of the vibrating movement that determines what level of reality the angel calls home.

The more refined the vibrational movement, the more levels of reality the angel is able to inter-penetrate.

Think on this for a moment. You will see how it is possible for what you perceive to be a high-ranking heavenly angel [such as Archangels Michael, Gabriel, and so on] to be able to move about freely into the denser levels of energy, and have a shining spot of their core matrix become a point of focus that is then able to radiate outwards and communicate in any direction through all the different layers of all realities. You will not see the full core or heart of these higher angels, but rather you will see and sense only the smallest projection of them.

As with myself, Ahale does not feel the full brunt of my personality. She tunes into the smallest speck of a much larger core personality. For those readers of a military mindset, liken an angel to a whole army moving through a countryside, yet from this massive army of unlimited numbers, a lone scout, a lone sapper will venture out from the main group and go alone into new areas. And like the lone scout that leaves the body of the main group, so is the part of me that works with Ahale.

This sliver of me is the scout, the sapper, the smaller piece of a much larger whole. And when this scouting work is done it retreats back to the main core. At any time, you in your physical reality will see the angelic scouts, these tendrils of a much greater personality that emanates out from the parent heart. Yet as the pen-wielding lady will tell you, even these scouts have a dramatic presence and the ability to rattle windows. It all depends on what the scouting or incursion is being done for, and this determines the strength and energy of this travelling gestalt. A big work in progress may mean a stronger focus from the angelic core. It truly depends on what is being accomplished.

Now, to confuse matters even more, these tendrils of the angelic core can become whatever shape or assume any disguise that it needs. Think of a lump of modelling clay; the main lump has its shape, and the small piece that is pinched off this main lump can become any shape it is worked into.

These splinter personalities can be seen, felt, and heard in myriad ways. And bear this in mind: the images or projections don't need to be always in a human form. These splinter holographic images can appear as one or more of a multitude of images, feelings, other creatures, wind, rain, heat, coldness, and even aliens.

The holographic angelic splinter may be of any images that boggle your mind, but it will be as it needs to be to carry out the successful completion of its intended mission. I smile at the word alien. Look up the word in your dictionaries. There are true aliens living amongst you. Everyone you call a stranger is, in fact, an alien.

A big goofy smile is floating around the room. The word alien seems to have a connection to a Samuel in-joke, and it helps make this a fun fact to think more about.

For example, you will all have heard stories of how an eagle swooped down and brought to someone's attention the correct path to take when they were dithering over which one they were meant to be on. Or the stranger who stopped someone in the street and in a few exchanged words changed their life for the better. You have all heard stories of what is known as angelic visits.

Now, the denizens of the natural worlds are very willing to do whatever they are able to do to help an angel friend, and so in the eagle example above, there is a partnership between a physical eagle and an angelic communicator, both working together towards a specific goal.

It will be very difficult for you to know without a shadow of doubt if you have had a true angelic visit, or a visit that was triggered by an angelic influence. I tell you truly, it does not matter in whatever shape or form any message comes to you. It is the message that is the important part, more so than the messenger. Although to twist more meaning into the fabric of the message, often the type of messenger can be an integral part of the message.

Have I confused you enough yet?

Angelic messengers may or may not be angelic personalities. Whatever the carrier, there will have been an angelic trigger of some sort. Messages may well be important enough to stand alone, yet at the same time you have to take into account the type of packaging that it came in, because this may give the message more depth and detail.

How is it possible to work out what is what and who is who? How is it possible to weave between all the what's and who's, and to work out exactly what is going on? I tell you truly, we can indeed be sneaky angels, because we may use plain truth or confusion as tools of message delivery; in fact, we happily use anything we deem effective to get the needed communication through to you.

We can use shock tactics, or we can use a gentle, loving nudging of the senses to help show someone a better way, or to put forward a new insight. We stir up the emotions, we smooth the emotions, we do what is needed, in whatever form, shape, or energy that is deemed to be needed for success.

Therefore, be prepared to see slivers of angels shimmering in the sunlight, or as a light flittering around in a darkened room just out of the corner of your eye, or as a stranger who asks you for some food, or maybe a hungry stray dog looking for a kindly home, or an eagle soaring overhead. Be ready for anything, anytime, anywhere.

Now we stop here, dearest daughter. It is a shorter session today.

The energy was coming through so strongly, so I was surprised to have the session not last as long as they usually do.

Well, we have begun this book with a lot of questions, haven't we? See, there is another one. The questions are an easy way to bring hidden concerns out into the open. What side of the seesaw do you want to sit on? Where, actually, is this seesaw that I keep talking about?

A curious reader will already have their list of questions piled up, and some may be such as these. Why do I have to do anything about anything, anyway? Why is it so important for me to make up my own mind? After all, other people can think things out better than I can.

Why do angels bother with me when I don't believe in them? Why can't the important messages from my higher self, or wherever they come from, come in a way that I can understand them, instead of coming in some weird symbolic language? And so forth.

Here now is a gentle reminder to you about the last question. You do understand the symbolic language. To remember this fact is one of the reasons you are down here on the earth in the first place. You need to remember in all ways, and within all experiences, just who you really are, while at the same time powering up your creative skills. So never tell me that you don't understand symbols. You know more of the spiritual language than you realise.

You know more about angels and spirit stuff than you may remember consciously at this time. You know more about everything. You may have deliberately shut down a lot of this deep knowledge, because it is a powerful knowing that can distress those who are not firmly balanced in all ways.

The total knowledge available to you is immense, but you may have chosen to work within a limited field so you are able to comfortably handle what you need to handle at this time.

Too much information all at once can confuse anyone, and this can make life-changing choices harder to work out, because the correct information you need at any given time may be like trying to find the needle in the proverbial haystack.

Almost an impossible task ... except for one factor. You have a needle-finding radar inside you, always switched on and ready to scan for the proverbial needle in the haystack. It goes by the name 'intuition' and this powerful tool also acts as a homing signal, so there is never a valid reason for you to say you cannot find your way in the world; nor can you say that you have diligently searched for the next signpost and were unable to find it – or that if you did find a sign that seemed to be appropriate, you were not able to read it.

You have a switched-on search machine and an automatic decoder in place and it's always ready to go to work on your behalf. The only reason you do not or have not understood your messages and signposts is that you have made a conscious choice to ignore them or put them to one side for now.

Maybe you have emotionally felt like doing something else instead of what you feel you are meant to be doing. On one level or another, at the time, you will have made a choice that you then discarded or ignored, or that you chose not to accept or understand any helpful input from, whatever the source.

Like the sun that comes up every morning over the horizon, so too does the God of your Inner You. You may only catch glimpses of this energy, this sparkly core, yet it is always there, always in position, always ready to rock and roll, and always traversing deep into the hidden realms within. And like the sun that spreads light across the land, when it reaches above the horizon this inner sparkly Creator energy spreads light across your inner and outer spaces.

When you connect with this all-powerful light, you will feel a surge of completeness, a surge of Love of All Things in such a massive manner that it literally takes your breath away. You will gasp with sheer pleasure and excitement. Your task is to now bring this inner sun into your everyday life, to lighten the darker patches, to bring joy and comforting light to wherever you travel on both your inner and outer journeys. This sun, this inner sun, is you as a being of light; but you already know this, don't you?

If you turn off all the lights on the darkest of nights, the ones with the eyes to see [third eye open] will see flares of the most brilliant light coming from each living thing. If you believe you are alive and kicking, then by all means see if you are able to discern these brilliant flares.

The light thus radiated truly lights up the world. The wordage describing the light is quite deliberate here, because how else can it be described? The light from the planet intermingles with the light that emanates from all its denizens and so lights up the universe. It is as a beacon of light in the wilderness. Know this, dear reader, and know it well; you are a part of a Beacon of Light that has a specific purpose to fulfil.

From where I stand, this beacon is the most amazing phenomenon, and the light pulsates with a rhythm of its own; it truly is a most magnificent sight, especially for this old angel. To watch this light cleansing away the darkness, to watch this light bring forth more balance and brilliance means that the planet and all included – within the animal, mineral, and vegetable kingdoms – is overcoming its earlier wobbles and gathering in strength and clarity towards a magical burst of brilliance. Oh, indeed, it makes me wax lyrical.

There has never been a dark age in the history of your planet. The dark ages in your so-called history books describe a short moment in time when the people did not want to think for themselves. They blinkered themselves in a very consciously controlled way. Of course, when the population got tired of playing this game, the dark ages came to an end.

Down through the various civilisations that have risen and then fallen, before your recorded history as well, there have been times that came and went as mankind played the blindfold game. But the true light was always within, patiently waiting to be noticed. Just imagine for a moment if someone has been wearing a blindfold for many lives, this person would get used to a certain level of darkness around themselves, materialising in such ways as the darkness of ignorance, or the lack of curiosity and hope.

Now imagine that one day in a moment of absent-mindedness, or because something at last pushed the curiosity button, the corner of the blindfold was lifted just that little bit. The light flooding in through the tiny opening would have been blindingly bright. It would have seemed miraculous, it would have seemed frightening, and it would have seemed to be godlike.

The contrast between what was known as normal with the blindfold in place and the new level of seeing would have been great. Like a blind man that could see for the first time. These images would have seemed jumbled and scary, while at the same time the emotions would have been soaring into ecstasy.

Just like a blinkered person removing a blindfold, so too is the sensation of touching and communing with the light of your inner God!

The Light is Creation, Light is Movement, Light is It.

3

BEINGS OF LIGHT —
THE HOLOGRAPHIC ROAD MAPS

*S amuel brings a lovely feeling of good humour and joy to the work ses-
sion this morning. It is a beautiful sensation when his energy floods
into the room like an unstoppable bow wave of energy, a vibrant energy
wave that makes everything awash with exhilarating and joyful energy. It's
a wonderful and magical way to start the day.*

Good day, dearest readers, I wish you all well, and at this
time we still talk about the Light. Yes, I know you may want
me to talk on another subject, such as interesting prophecies,
or pixies and goblins, but even these little ones depend on
light vibrations for their form, their reality, their existence,
as do you.

The light vibration we speak of today is not on a single
vibrational level but the multi levels, the multi functioning of
the light. The world you see around you is made up of light
energy. This you know from what I have said already, and it is
the density, rapidity, rotation, and strength of each vibrational
light strand that makes you what you are and makes your world
what it is.

You cannot get away from the subject of light because you
are a being of light! You cannot get away from yourself. It is

you, it is the breath of God, so bear with me for a short time while I try to make the day-to-day connections easier for you to see. You are a spark of light that lives amongst a whole Universe of Light.

First, close your eyes and imagine this: unlimited dancing, swirling lights of all shapes and sizes, all flowing around each other, between, into, and out of each other, yet never colliding with a forceful impact. Well, sometimes that does happen, but that is for another time and another session, because it is not a frequent occurrence.

The dancing lights are like fireflies, the lightning bugs that illuminate a dark corner of the night with their swirling lights. It is like a starry night blossoming into full movement.

I will briefly describe the view we see from our reality like this: we may look down upon a crowded city plaza where all the people are jammed shoulder to shoulder while listening to an orator doing his spiel from a raised platform. We see this crowd as a densely packed collection of individual and collective lights. Some people's light shines brighter and clearer than others and some people have lights that flare brightly enough to lighten up their patch in the crowd.

Others may have a dull or flickering radiance around them that, in fact, draws energy from the stronger people in the crowd near them. So, we can see each individual energy essence or light body intermingling with everyone else's body of light. We see each shining personal core with its essential connection to everything and everyone else.

We see the Godhead, the energetic shields, the charkas, the inner and outer core, all the points of spiritual light, all points of light that make up an individual person. And then we see the crowd as a whole, the collective light of the crowd.

This magical light is made up of an intermingling of all the light densities that come from each individual. We can see immediately if this is a happy crowd, a concerned crowd, an angry crowd, or a jubilant one. We can see if there is someone amongst this crowd who will have the potential to influence it as a whole. We can see immediately where the most troublesome factors are.

To see the light emanating from a crowd, such as I have described, allows us, you, or anyone, to read the crowd as it really is.

Now imagine a family group together in the same room. Imagine yourself as a spirit, hovering above this family group. Your spirit self is looking down from near the ceiling, but your body is still sitting in the lounge chair. Your focus or seeing eye is looking down on the full family gathering.

From this vantage point, the spirit of you will be able to see and understand so much information about the group dynamics. You will see the differences in the light that radiates from each family member, and you will be able to see clearly whether the family acts as a cohesive unit or as a fractured, scattered, and non-communicating unit.

You will instantly be able to see by the light patterns how each family member reacts to another in a real sense. Is the light that embraces two people smooth and beautifully flowing, or are there jagged spikes flaring and flashing between them? Just a general note inserted here, many of the readers will know about the aura, the energy light field, and the readings that clairvoyant and psychic practitioners do, so they will know of the light connections between souls.

This aura light is, of course, a part of what I am speaking about. But there are more levels of light interaction between people and everything else in existence that have never been documented during this current time. The surface information on this subject has barely been scratched.

As more people train themselves to see the different layers of the light vibrations, more information about these levels will gradually become shared with the metaphysically interested people. When anyone does see the energy fields, they are touching briefly on a tiny spectrum of a most magnificent whole.

Now, do not be disappointed if you cannot immediately grasp the full ramification of what I have just said. In time, everyone will know that humans and, of course, all others are beings made of light energy. This is not just semantics, or a way of describing something that is future knowledge but is, in fact, the truth. In the fullness of time, everyone will understand the word **enlightenment** in a more comprehensive way.

So, bear with me. I am not putting down the talents of aura readers or talented intuitive people of all ilks. All I am saying is that in time, they will realise that what they are seeing now is just the tiniest fragment of a peek into an Aladdin's Cave.

Now, back to the family group. As a hovering eye focusing from near the ceiling and looking downwards, you will see the family unit both as a whole and as individual personalities. Blend all this mixed light, stir it all together well, and then add in all the light that is emanating from the furniture, the house, and all its fixtures. Stir well.

Add in the light from the geographical aspects of the surrounding area. Stir well. Then add to this light mix, the light from the earth, moon, all the stars, all the sky lights. Mix all these light sources together well and add this to the general mix.

You will quickly see that the sources of light are unlimited, because they go on and on ad infinitum. What a wonderful way to see people, to read them, and to connect with them. And by the way, do not forget to add to the mix, the light of your spirit splinter focus, from your position overlooking the family.

There is a lot of good-humoured banter and jollity coming through in these paragraphs and it is harmoniously, beautifully, and gently being mixed into the ambience of the room. Samuel has just described an interesting family dynamic!

Do you see angels looking over everyone's shoulders? Then add their light to the mix.

These are two small examples. You probably need to let your imagination loose on this idea, because in everyday life, you are so used to looking at things with your physical eyes that you see only in a limited range of light.

Now, you instinctively know that I speak the truth here, because other creatures living on the planet have different ranges of vision to what you possess. Some creatures see well at night; some don't. Some creatures see better in very bright light, and some don't. Therefore, you know there are light spectrums that you cannot see with your physical eyes.

Allow your imagination to put you in the middle of the Soup of Light and see it all swirling around you. See this wonder with your third eye, your Spirit Eye. You will find it an enriching and rewarding exercise to do when you have the time and quietness to allow yourself to fly away uninterrupted, into the fields of light.

You will not get lost amongst the majesty, because you have a homing beacon going thump, thump, thump inside you that will always draw the focus back home, from anywhere, anytime, or any place.

And with that, the swirling signature of Samuel indicated that the book dictation session was over for the morning. It was quite a fun time for me, and the words and imagery coming through with the dictation were strong and uplifting. The visionary film clips behind my eyelids showing groups of soup-stirring cooks, gleefully throwing stuff into the pot, are quite comical.

Good day, dearest daughter. This chapter is not quite finished, so away we go.

The family unit is a good place to practice seeing the lights we are talking about, because family members are usually close by and in changeable moods and emotions on a regular basis. Therefore, you will get the opportunity to see in an immediate way how the emotions alter the light patterns around a person at least on one level or another.

If you don't feel you can pry into your family's state of being, then go out into public places and see what light you can see or sense around strangers. Do not feel you are prying without permission, because you will only be allowed to see what both you and the subject, whether family or strangers, have unconsciously agreed to allow you to see. This is a sort of spontaneous communication between people on a deep and intimate level.

As I have said, there will be many more layers of light found by metaphysical researchers. Over time, the road maps that show how everything is connected by energy will begin to emerge. Even now, in your present time, there are people who are seeing new patterns and new connections but have not yet shown these to the public.

A note of interest here: some of the earlier civilisations had road maps of different light patterns and levels, some levels of the light being seen clearly and recorded well. As an example, I suggest that the ancient Chinese knew and worked very well with the multiple layers of light they could see, on what you now know to be the acupuncture and nadi systems.

Other cultures had other specialisations. Much of this older knowledge has been lost and misplaced in the mists of time and the rush of today, but what will newly emerge in your present time will be a more comprehensive Map of Light.

More of the light levels will be slotted together and the road maps will be seen by the students of metaphysics in its holographic nature. This is the uplifting time when human-kind is supposed to be bringing forth the previously hidden, forgotten, and unused insights about enlightenment, and the vibrational rising towards perfect evolution. And this knowledge most definitely includes who and what a person truly is.

A Being of Light.

Now I say this to you, beautiful reader, do not be dazzled by the knowledge that is coming through via metaphysical researchers and practitioners. Please don't accept everything stated as fact or even as fiction. Take all new ideas into your thoughts, then only delve into what your intuition says is comfortable for you to work with, because even the best-intentioned person will only be putting forth his or her personal interpretation of what they believe to be the truth. It is when this new knowledge comes through in a consistent way, with even more people intuitively checking it out, that the fuller and more rounded picture may emerge.

Imagine for a moment that you can see a room that is full to the ceiling, full of knowledge and information about 'light' and light bodies in all their various forms. This room has multiple doors and windows. Each metaphysical researcher will be peeking through one door or one window, and they will see only what is to be seen from the specific angle they are looking from.

As more people peek through other doors and windows, a fuller picture can be pieced together, despite the fact that the light within the room is billowing and swirling, dancing and twinkling in non-stop action. And remember, all this action is only happening in the imagination of these onlookers, because the fact is that the room cannot truly contain the light in any way. This is an interesting exercise in patience upon patience.

So, are you now clear on the simple description of what you really look like? Light, multi-layered, dancing, changing, and vibrating light.

The next step is to activate this information. You now know you are a being of light; and so, what are you supposed to do about it? Turn the light switch off so you don't waste any power? Cover the glowing light so that you hide your true self from the scrutiny of others?

Many people try this action, and they go to the most extraordinary lengths to stop people seeing into their inner selves and their true personality. Invariably, these secretive people are so locked into their belief of showing only what they allow others to see and judge them by, they partly camouflage their physical selves as well.

They don't know or believe in the light body, but this camouflaged person has failed in his or her attempt to block the people with the eyes to see from seeing their true nature and have actually hidden nothing, despite all the covering applied.

The essence of personality wriggles from beneath the applied covers, whether they be physical, emotional, mental, or attempted spiritual manipulations, and shines forth like a beacon. So much effort would have been expended creating uniforms, masks, or deliberately misleading actions that may fool only some of the people, some of the time. And this is not a smart way to expend whatever personal energy is available.

What are you actually supposed to do with this knowledge about your personal light body?

Answer: look and see what your personal light brings to light.

There is a wonderful display of moving lights dancing, all cavorting gleefully around other lights that are dancing around even more energised lights, on my visionary cinema screen. There is such a joyful and exhilarating feeling dancing along with the strands of energy and power. It is almost blinding in radiance, and I love it all. I want to giggle with sheer undiluted delight at what I am seeing.

You don't need to go searching for things to do with these newly learned or remembered truths. The light will show you things that are already in place before your eyes but were previously unseen. These 'things to do' and 'things to know' have been there all along, patiently waiting for you to notice them and focus your attention on them.

In the future, the blending of the multiples of light will bring forth a new inner landscape that will transcend anything you have seen thus far. There will be a new sense of bonding between all living entities; there will be a new cohesiveness of collective ambitions, and of collective planning. There will be an opening up of the spectrum of realities that you can access more easily. That last sentence says it all – and now it is a good time for you to take a coffee break.

The session was finished with a personal word, and some deep insights were given on a family matter that was concerning me. This also turned out to be the end of Chapter 3.

4

TICK-TOCK TIME —
COFFEE FILTERS AND THE
EVOLUTIONARY LADDER

So that you understand in greater detail the future human-kind is heading towards, let me give you extra information on this interesting time. As a species, you are gradually heading for an existence without the physical coat that is an integral part of your makeup in this turn of the wheel.

You will still be you, but with 'you' as an energy gestalt that is able to transcend many layers of reality, while you are within your light body. You will still reside in a more or less specific level of vibrational energy. Just because you have successfully graduated from your physical reality level, does not mean you never need to learn anything again.

You will still be climbing on the evolutionary ladder but in a different sphere of activity, and using a different focus, and having different adventures. The essence of you is never going to be stuck in a rut or remain in a static place forever, because that has never been the plan.

When you have succeeded in understanding the manipulation of energy in one reality, you will have the choice to move on to and into another reality, or you will have the choice to stay and assist those coming behind you and help them step up into a new existence. Now, we are not talking in years or even decades here, so please understand this … the timing is not 'tick-tock time' related.

Time as you know it, your tick-tock time, does not exist in the true sense of time. When I say I do not speak of time in the scale of years, I mean it to be exactly that. When you leave behind the constraints of your physical cloak, a new panorama will blossom before you, and you will begin to remember the total expansiveness of the vibrational levels.

Also, you will begin to remember the power of thought and instant creation. You will begin to remember a Love of All Things that is so profound, it will knock your non-existent socks off.

You are heading towards the 'time' when in all ways, you will truly understand you are creating your own reality, with all its unlimited connections. In this physical world, you have an ideal setting to create in and then visibly show yourself the outcome of any creative endeavour. This is the slower, grosser level that allows you time to see and understand what it is you are doing.

Unfortunately, some individuals and institutions have taken the incentive and knowledge of your creativity away from you, or you voluntarily gave this power away to the ones who wanted it more than you. Therefore, you may struggle to see the big picture point of your current existence because the goal posts have been moved.

The rule book will have also been deliberately altered by the power seekers. This is because often the power games are being played in secrecy and darkness, and it is harder to see the full picture.

Lo and behold! What comes next?

Enlightenment.

Are you beginning to get the full idea of what I am saying this word truly means? The light gets turned on so that you can see and understand where you are, and what you are meant to be doing. Lo and behold, universal help is always there in one way or another for you to become aware of, and to help you relearn, all needed knowledge.

Lo and behold, a new and knowledgeable you can then emerge into the present. If you stubbornly and with ill nature refuse to accept or even acknowledge any enlightened insights that are put before you, you will stay in a state of stasis, which is a place of powerlessness and fear.

Please never allow this back-slipping and fearful action to take place, because, after all, you are a warrior who deserves the best of everything. Once you have placed one foot on the ladder that leads towards the light of evolution, don't look back or stop to gaze idly around you.

Focus your attention strongly on the next step and become confident that you will make this destination with surety and strength. The next step will always seem to be a huge step, but remember it is not a test or an examination where you need to get a certain score before you pass. It is a **doing** step, an action that is for your highest benefit and growth.

The more steps you are able to accomplish, the easier you will understand your current place in the spiritual hierarchies and find it easier to use your intuitive abilities to make the most of any situation that empowers your personal power pack into greatness.

At this point, I am thinking thank goodness for the imagery of stepping up on the rungs of a ladder. It is a simple imagery and one that everyone understands. This comment does not fit in with the context of 'light evolution' in a physical way, but the imagery, the example, the analogy is so simple, classy, and exact.

You ascend a ladder step by step; you ascend through the different vibrational levels step by step. And right now, I will also add, the word ascension is not totally correct in the context of the evolution topic, because the next realities are not always in the 'up' direction as you know it. I am being pedantic here and trying to be as accurate as I can with a subject that by its very nature is difficult to describe accurately in a few words.

I think Samuel is having a fun, wry dig at himself here because he is not a spirit of a few words. Rather, he is a spirit of many words and insightful commentary. He can be very sneaky with how he hides insightful information in non-challenging sentences.

In fact, the words may be ordinary and everyday ones that make up the sentences, but later when you are thinking about what you have read, little multiple pops of "ah ha" bubble into your thoughts, when a conscious understanding of Samuel's information is triggered. As I go about my daily tasks, I frequently get new insights about what was written in the morning dictation, and they really are "ah ha" moments.

The 'up' gives you an instant image of rising above so that you can see the bigger picture, and the 'climbing the ladder' analogy is perfect for this.

Let curiosity take you to where the rungs of this ladder of ascension are to be found. Let the understanding of your next evolutionary step strengthen and become even clearer and stronger with each tiny sliver of light you allow into your darkest area.

You do not have to fuss and worry about the ladder, or about what I call the big picture aspects and what is involved, or who you will be and what you will have to do on these next levels. You need to concentrate fully on where you are **now** and keep your senses open to the presence of the higher, yet different vibrational entities, who will always be of immense help to you right **now**.

You don't need to know what God or what Angel sits 'ruling' over which spiritual level, or the price of admission to the spiritual level after this current one. You don't need to know any details. From where you are standing, there is a good chance that even with the details out in the open, you will not be able to see clearly enough to understand anything and it will not make any type of sense to you.

You know, and I know, that individuals can and do visit the realms that are closest to them. They do incursions, forays, and quick and fast fact-finding trips; and when the results of these trips are told to others, this brings information, ideas and imageries of what exists in these next levels into play.

Note, for example, the phrase 'astral travelling'. I am sure you have heard it somewhere along the way. To astral travel means that you travel into areas that are usually unknown to you, and not the familiar areas you consider to be local. You travel into other levels and areas of existence.

Of course, at this point we need to mention the dream state and deep meditation states; these are familiar states and would be classed in this instance as local despite the varied destinations reached. Some people remember their journeys into the deep non-physical worlds, and so a gradual picture of these realms is built up over time.

However, despite whatever destinations these inner travels reach, there is always the connective tie, the grounding anchor held firmly into the physical reality. This grounding or connection is always there, and the inner landscapes that you travel through will have the sheen of your physical reality over the imagery.

It is not so much what is seen on these travels that is the interesting factor, because you need to remember that this grounding anchor does make a difference in how you interpret what you see in your travels. You are looking through a patina of physicalness with your specific beliefs and learned knowledge.

In other words, no matter what you see and do in the next levels of inner travelling, you will interpret them personally, how a soul tied to a specific physical body will interpret them.

This is not a put down in any way of these intrepid inner travellers who have brought so much information back from their forays. Indeed, they are taking the right action because this is how curiosity is guiding and immersing humankind in the Light of the Creator. It is just that the human conscious mind has a unique mind of its own and interprets everything through this uniqueness, and this personally colours any insights that come bubbling up from the subconscious.

This is just something to think about, so I offer a quick example right here. My words come from a reality not far away, and how these words are placed on the page is coloured by the mind of the person wielding the pen, even though most of this person's focus is pushed aside to allow room for my energy to come through.

Ultimately, it is through her energy that the words flow onto the page. So, there will be a slight change from my end of the line to her receiving end of the production line. Just imagine the words coming through many filters, filters of energy that have graduations of fineness.

Imagine this filter going backwards; the words come with fineness and clarity from me then go through coarser and coarser filtration until they land, plop, on the paper.

There is a big chuckle and a real sense of fun coming through all the 'filters' from Samuel to me.

The ensuing interpretation is similar, but the subtleties may be filtered out. That is a fact that comes from living where you do in the physical world. The dream state has less filtering going on.

In the physical world, coffee is coffee despite the degree of filtration, and there is no alteration of the basic structure. Actually, while I am talking about coffee, even the coffee pot may be used as a simple analogy because moving between realities corresponds to the coffee moving between filters. If you wish to visit the Higher Realms, you need to become fine enough to pass through all the filtration units. Think on this. The finer particles can flow down through the coarser levels if they choose to do so, but not so the other way around.

Do you still want to know why you are doing all these learning and enlightenment exercises and having interesting experiences in the first place? Because at this point, and despite my many words, you may have already forgotten what has been explained so far, and if this is so, then here is a gentle reminder for you now. It is simply because you are learning to manipulate energy, to make, to create, and to love who you are while you are doing these activities.

You are taking the opportunity to have a most wonderful journey towards Home, enjoying all the side trips, all events, all fellow travellers, and all experiences that come your way. You are living, you are a Spark of the Creator, and you are at one with this journeying.

Hey there, why not make the most of your time and energy? You are committed to this odyssey whether you like it or not at this time on the Wheel of Life, so, you may as well make it an enjoyable journey. Do what you can to make this life count for something enriching and magnificent. You know it counts already, but it is you who will be the arbitrator in the final counting whether to place this life as a positive one or as a less positive one.

Now, the essence of this movement or journey, in a very basic sense, is actually the action of moving.

When a play on a word appears on the page, it is usually accompanied by wry, tongue-in-cheek energy. In this case, Samuel is injecting a great feeling of fun into the conversation and I'm not sure where he is going with this.

You now know that everything in existence is made up of moving molecules, and if you do not believe me, then believe your scientists. The moving energy creates patterns; the patterns create shapes; the shapes manifest as whatever you wish them to manifest as.

And so, your movement or journey through various experiences in this lifetime and other lifetimes is not a random movement but a deliberate patterning of light molecules. You have a destination in mind at all times, but you will enjoy the detours and exciting opportunities that come your way as you explore along the byways and highways that you come across.

Imagine a dressmaker firstly thinking up the way the dress will look when finished, then deciding on the materials, the colours, the needed sizes, and so on. Secondly, imagine the cutting of the pattern shapes, then the cutting of the material to fit these paper shapes. Thirdly, imagine the material pieces being sewn together to make the dress.

That sequence is the grand plan, but this dressmaker tries to see if any other style options will suit the final product better than the one selected. The dressmaker will try different colour combinations, will maybe alter a sleeve length or even try a different bias to the cut of the fabric.

These are little detours, detours of questing, and it does not matter how many possible changes are made, because the final goal is the creation of a dress. The side efforts have added excitement and experience to the dressmaker's repertoire because he or she will have been squirreling away the checks and balances of each choice as they were investigated.

So, we do have total freedom to make both patterns and pattern changes, up to a certain point. There would be little sense for the dressmaker to go radically outside the image of what is a dress, to make a dress.

If you are heading towards the understanding that you are a being of light, then you do things that keep you heading in the general direction of this understanding. You don't just randomly turn yourself into a jar of honey and get stuck on the shelf in someone's pantry … or worse! You may be an enlightened jar of honey but stuck in a cupboard you surely will be.

Therefore, along the journey, it is very acceptable to make alterations to your patterning choices, but the final goal needs to be kept firmly in mind at all times.

This is so much fun, because as the above words were being dictated, I could 'see' the jar of honey on a shelf desperately shuffling into the furthest corner, away from the hand that was reaching for it.

It's not a pleasant feeling if you find yourself dominated by someone with a strong willpower or presence. And dominated so strongly that you can obviously see and acknowledge to yourself that you have surrendered or lost your power of choice.

Why bring this oddball comment up now? Because the anxious honey in the jar is being dominated by the intentions of the hungry consumer and is not enjoying life as a peaceful jar of honey. You need to be strong and steady and give yourself all the confidence you need to put yourself in the optimum position to make the choices you want to make and not be coerced by anyone else. If you feel unable to do this, start the ball rolling by deciding to change one small thing in your life.

To make things even easier for yourself, go quietly and sneakily about changing the situation of feeling not in control, by determinedly doing one thing that **you** want to do. One little thing at a time. You see, it is not the dominance or the control that someone has over you physically that is the over-riding factor here; the critical point is the inner freedom and strength you have by not allowing others to have control over your inner creativity.

You can be a prisoner in a cold, dark dungeon, yet still be in control of who you really are. This is not science fiction. Your literature has many references and stories about great men and women who were able to overcome the most frightful depredation, and triumph into greatness because of their inner strength and adherence to reaching their personal goals.

The inner strength, the inner creativity is a formidable power, so never feel that you are not good enough to personally decide how to work things out and decide how you wish to react with anyone, or anything. Alter your belief patterns if they need to be changed to achieve personal success of any sort. It is all about your choices.

Hey, making or tweaking patterns, or creating anything, is living. It's all as simple as that. The patterns or ground plans you make in your everyday living become as tiny glowing specks of light, that then unite and intermingle with all other patterns, plans, attempts, and activities to form a blueprint for action; and this blueprint for action needs to be able to advance you towards the next evolutionary step that you are in the process of taking.

Dearest daughter, this is Chapter 4 finished. We will leave the start of the next chapter until the next session. I now bid you a very good morning.

The session finished with the swirling signature of Samuel. This was quite a fun book dictation, because I was getting a lot of the comical images that came with the words, like the jar of honey trying to hide from the creeping hand; or the bright little drop of personality that was sliding joyfully though the coffee filters, having a great time riding the slippery path down into different reality levels. Or the dressmaker making so many practice runs with different materials that she or he buries themself under a pile of fabric, with hands poking out of the top of the pile trying to get their bearings of what is up and what is down.

Actually, as the words come in all the book dictation sessions, these images or visions flow right along with the words, and some sessions are quite hilarious for me. Yet, I know that this is not always coming out on the page. Samuel does appear to have a well-developed sense of humour and a keen sense of the ridiculous, and I realise that I am not getting everything that is being offered down. In fact, I'm picking up only the tiniest fraction of what is available to 'catch'.

But whatever I catch, I love it! I can be sitting at the table with my hand busily writing and trying to keep up with what Samuel is offering, when the ridiculousness of the cartoon strip images hits me, and I burst into giggles.

5

LAUGHTER AND LEMONS

I t is eleven days since the last book dictation, and despite my good intentions, daily life activities have seemed to take over. At the same time, I have been trying to catch up with the first typing of the earlier "An Angel Speaks" sessions. My typing is a one-finger effort and is still slow and cumbersome. I'm still very much a learner of typing and word processing.

In this last week or so, there have been many interesting things happening; coincidences galore, synchronistic happenings coming out of the woodwork, spontaneous therapy sessions with friends, interesting family news, more gentle and very welcome rain falling in the area, and the opportunity to use some of the predictive visions that have been popping into my thoughts, all with great results.

I have not forgotten about the book sessions, but there were days when I forgot to bring the manuscript with me, or I would unintentionally leave it behind, either at my place of living, or at the clinic where I am able to use a small room for my work.

Samuel is not absent from my life while these mini breaks in dictation occur. He freely has his say during the daily personal journal entries, and is always giving advice if needed, encouragement, or offering pithy comments about events that are happening or are yet to happen. While this is going on, there seems to be a building up of something under the surface *of my daily activities, or a speeding up of something. And I must say, I am curious.*

Good day, dearest daughter. Put the heading for this chapter as Laughter and Lemons. This title has a nice lilt to it, don't you feel?

A good day to you, dear readers.

And I start with the question, what have you laughed at, or with, today? Oh dear, you have found nothing to laugh about yet? That is not acceptable. Well, do not despair, because to run the full gamut of emotions means that now and again you will be in an unhappy state.

You may briefly flit through darker moods like depression, sadness, or unhappiness, before raising your emotional levels towards happiness, laughter, wellbeing, or any other fun and light-hearted feeling. You have previously read my words about the need for everything to be balanced, and laughter and gloominess are both a part of an emotional balance that needs to find creative expressive outlets in your life.

Don't get me wrong; to laugh and to laugh a lot is great, and I will speak more on this, but, if you see someone who is always laughing, always giggling and carrying on even in unfunny situations, you will eventually wonder, "What is wrong with this person? What is he or she trying to hide, or not wanting to deal with?"

And this would be an insightful observation for you. Laughter is the outward expression of good humour, but to laugh most hours of the day does make a witness wonder if there is something being hidden by this action.

Ah ha, I think I just caught a question in Ahale's thoughts. She thought, "I wonder where this is going?"

He did catch this fleeting thought, because I had just idly wondered where Samuel was going with this subject.

I am not going far. In fact, I am not going anywhere. I stay right here and say this: it doesn't matter if someone you know is a jolly person, who always sees the upbeat side of things, who is an incredible optimist and will laugh and joke at all times, or who in each hour of every day, determinedly sees the comical side of life.

Look under the facade of the constant jollity that is being presented to others. Someone who is always upbeat and laughing without stop is invariably covering up a degree of inner disharmony, a sense of inner disquiet and discontent.

If you do not believe me, look closely at some of your well-known comedians past and present. Many have had tragically repressive private lives, and this is a side of them that they generally wish to keep well-hidden. It is almost as though too much of one thing triggers a reversal of emotions deep within, and so the balance between the laughter and gloom loses cohesion. The distance between the outlets of these emotions becomes wider apart and unstable in activity.

So, laughter and good fellowship is a beautiful and wonderful combination. Note well who has a balanced sense of humour and note well who has not. Incessant laughter and contrived good humour are often an effective shielding of inner disharmony.

Why am I telling you this?

I tell you to remind you that even good guys, or happy guys, could have camouflaged levels of disharmony that may or may not be too deeply hidden. You need to enjoy the humour that the comedians or upbeat people offer you, but at the same time you need to be sensitive enough to work out if this humour is being used as a camouflage projection, so everyone is distracted from seeing the true persona beneath.

Again, it is the old adage: "Do not judge a book by its cover."

That says it all quite succinctly.

So, what are some of the camouflage personalities or faces that people can project? What is one false face that you can quickly think of?

Here are one or two as quick examples.

The pious demeanour of a do-good person, who beneath all the spouted words is really a bigot, narrow minded and intolerant of others. Or a housewife who keeps her house spotless and is so fanatical about this spotlessness that her family is cowed and afraid to be spontaneous or enjoy life in any way.

This controlling behaviour shows the true demeanour of a person who is afraid to enjoy life themselves. And so, they try to keep this self-knowledge to themselves, so others do not see their fear. Yet it will not remain hidden and will creep out into the light of day, despite all efforts to keep this inner fear deeply controlled and concealed.

Maybe you know a man who is surrounded by the trappings of wealth, and he surrounds himself with all the luxuries that money can buy ... homes, works of art, and many vehicles and travelling devices; in fact, whatever he deems luxury items to be. Yet deep within he has a paucity of generosity and compassion in his make up, and that information he doesn't want anyone to know, so he hides this knowledge about himself with the luxury items that are placed front and centre as a shield between himself and others.

The do-gooder uses many pious words as a cover. Listen to what I say; not watch what I do. The housewife uses the super-clean house as a cover. Look at my clean house; don't look closely at me.

The wealthy man uses luxury things as a cover. Look what I own; don't inspect my personality.

All have put into place a façade, a false front that is intended to hide from other people some sort of inner lack, intolerance, fear, or a feeling of inadequacy. For example, the personally unhappy comedian who uses laughter as a camouflaging tool is activating a false front.

Look at your fellow citizens with new eyes, look beneath the projected public persona and sense what is going on inside their personal character makeup. Do not take everything you see at face value, because any active façade is a vested output of energy on the part of the originator. And they will not be happy about having their carefully constructed shielding penetrated in any way.

There is a gentle feeling of what I can only describe as whimsical humour embedded in these words. Whimsical humour is a strange description here, but it fits with what Samuel is writing.

The words about 'not being happy' seem to be the key here. And he indicates, with gentle humour, the conundrum of having what is thought to be a secure screen hiding personal traits that are meant to remain hidden, yet which are very easily seen despite all the shoring up of defences.

To get to know this person, you need to see beneath this camouflage, and this is where your intuitive responses are critically important, because you really need to know who to trust, who is being dishonest, who is concealing their true motives, and so forth. You need to know the true nature of the person you are walking besides, and who you can rely on in all ways and, also, who you are together with as you climb on the evolutionary ladder.

To naively believe everything you are told, especially about untruthful situations by people who are misleading, and whether this misleading is being done in a deliberate or an unconscious manner, means that you are yet to find your truth. You are yet to become confident in yourself, confident enough that you can choose what, where, and when you need to do anything.

Laughter can be used as such an effective screening device, and it is in your best, your very best interest, to intuit whether the laughter you hear comes from true humour or is being used to cover and conceal true motives. As you learn to intuit and then understand when these contrived covers are in place, you may find that you will continue to enjoy the fun and good humour that is being projected, but compassion and a deeper understanding will creep in to your mind. And a new scenario is born.

This scenario shows that you are being presented with a choice you must make. Do you, or do you not, connect with this person on a level that will send an empathic bolt of good will and compassionate understanding into the heart of the performer? Of course you do, and by the way, the performer will know that you have sent this energy. Do not doubt that in any way.

It may not be a conscious knowing, but the performer's intuitive self will feel the connection. See, without even trying, you will have helped bring a little more balance into an unstable or awkward situation.

I can hear you saying, "Samuel, not everyone is so overboard with this camouflaging, so why are you talking so much about it?"

I say to these people, there is more dishonest camouflaging going on around you than you realise. Fear and fearful beliefs are prevalent, especially prevalent the higher the
living standards of any given civilisation. Can you say that
you know a totally honest person, a person who expresses
thoughts and emotions in a totally and always truthful
manner?

Little children are more likely to blurt out what they feel,
and they will do this until it is drummed into them not to be
too open and frank with their comments.

The sad part of all this is that the person who tries to
hide their true inner emotions or nature, often comes to consciously believe that the camouflage suit they have carefully
constructed is a true reflection of their personality. And when
this happens, a deep chasm or a wider conflict of warring emotions will destabilise the internal balance even more.

Look through the façade of others.

Then look through your own.

Ah ha. Now comes the hard part, because here comes the
word honesty. It is now time for you to get to work in uncovering and removing the layers, the trappings, and any scaffold-
ing that you may have unintentionally been hiding behind. If
you have any secret fears, phobias, or uncertainties that you
have kept hidden from other people, why not decide to do
something about these hidden concerns?

After all, you must be expending time and energy making
sure you keep yourself vigilant enough to not allow anyone to
peep into your emotional closet of hidden skeletons. Decide
to take these deep, dark secrets out of the box, however small
and insignificant they may be, and bring them into the light so
you may see clearly what it is you have been hiding all these

years. Then deal with them as the intelligent, Galactic citizen that you are.

If these hidden secrets have been stashed away for quite some time, when you bring them out into the open you will probably find that the original secret phobia, or fear, is not quite as you remember it to be.

Think back on how you remembered things as a child, and how you remember things as you are now. There will be a great difference between the two versions. So, it stands to reason that when you uncover your secret 'secret' you may not even recognise it for what you think it represents.

Memory changes over time, and it is your conscious filing system having many outside distractions to cope with that has doggedly kept your phobias and deepest secrets in the rut of your darkest thoughts.

Lighten up. Give yourself a break. Break apart your box of phobias, look at them, understand them for what they represent, and then let them free. Let them be free to fly away and transmute into the light.

The load on your shoulders will lighten, because these inner kept secrets are heavy to carry around. Lighten your load. Let them be free.

6

WOBBLY WARRIORS —
TWO STEPS FORWARD AND
ONE STEP BACK
AUDIENCE PARTICIPATION

The path of the budding Warrior of Light is littered with hazards that can cause detours to pop up unexpectedly and make the seeker stumble. The seeker will have to hop, skip, and jump over, around, under, or through the obstacles that are placed randomly on their Path of Life.

The budding Warrior needs to keep the end goal firmly in mind, yet still concentrate fully on whatever is being done, or experienced, in their now time. To a certain degree, how you approach or venture into this obstacle course will make a huge difference to the final outcome. It depends a lot on the mindset, the determination, the level of faith, and the clarity of belief that the intrepid traveller holds deeply within.

Now, don't feel you have to become a steely-eyed, no-nonsense, dogmatic warrior who tramples over everything to reach the end goal of completing this warrior course ... which, in fact, is the journey towards enlightenment and Home. No, of course you do not.

You can waffle, you can side step, you can change your mind, you can flipper, flapper, and falter at all points along the way, and you can be as indecisive as you like, but understand this; the clearer you are in your intent to live a Godly life, the clearer and firmer you will be during the learning that comes from walking the warrior path, and ultimately, when understanding the bigger Universal Picture.

The clearer and more concise the intent, the brighter the Light of Love will shine on your path of destiny, thus enabling you to see the better options to choose from, or at the very least, allowing you better visibility while you are detouring around obstacles.

Therefore, even if you are one of the people who do waffle around, or one of the people who take two steps forward then one step back, you will still slowly and surely increase your understanding of what it means to be alive and kicking. The two steps forward [increasing the light] is making it all happen for you, while the one step backwards does not take away the inner radiance from the forward steps. Mind you, as you take the backward step your inner light may dim ever so slightly. It may become less 'bright', but it will not be lost.

This inner light you can call love, hope, or the Creative Spark, you can take your pick on what you name this personal signature. To remind everyone, I am not talking literally about a light wattage here, as in candle power or horsepower. I am definitely talking about the wattage of God power, the inner God of you. It is the gradual accumulation of all the bits and pieces of insights and understandings that come into your personal space that brings this inner light into a solid and clear brightness, or into the brightness of a prism of scattered pieces that are together, but not yet melded into a cohesive unit.

Let all the words come and go. What I say will not make any difference to how your inner light is programmed, and this is fact. The only thing that controls your light switch, your dimmer or brightness switch, is you personally.

You may read words of wisdom until your eyes drop from their sockets or until the lost pet bird flies back to its cage, and you can read so many metaphysical books that you become a very well-read person, but doing all this does not necessarily change your level of inner light. You need to act, to do something enlightened enough to adjust this inner light switch and strengthen the Light.

The osmosis of ideas will not move this level. Rather, there needs to be an action that is energised and instigated by you, and only then will you alter your inner landscape.

Now you may disagree with what has just been said – but hear me out. For example, imagine that you have decided to attend a seminar where the main speaker on the dais promises to lighten and cleanse your aura or energetic body, and will show you how to heal someone after this cleansing and attunement has been done. This is not an uncommon example, and you will see this type of seminar advertised in your local media outlets. After a day of listening to the theory behind the speaker's techniques, you decide to go ahead and be cleansed or attuned so that you may become a healer.

It is now your turn to sit in the special chair while the practitioner does whatever needs to be done to cleanse or attune you to the correct degree. The necessary movements will be done over you, while you sit placidly and idly on the chair.

Actually, you were not entirely idle because you had a few quick thoughts about how you were going to handle the peak hour traffic when you were driving home, or maybe you began wondering, albeit briefly, about what you could cook for the evening meal. You were focusing on something other than what was going on around you.

Do you feel that the practitioner did the job that was promised? Do you feel that you have now changed enough that you can get up out of the chair, feeling like a new, clean, and fully attuned you? Of course not, because you have not connected with what was happening, even though you sat willingly enough in the chair. You were not fully committed to the process at hand.

You needed to make a total connection to the procedural action; you needed, on a conscious and intuitive level, to give yourself permission to fully open yourself to what was happening, and to fully accept all the ensuing consequences of these actions. You had to make a decision and stick with it! You had to become a fully aware and participating participant of the ongoing procedure.

You see, no one can do anything to you without your express permission. No one can do anything to you without your co-operation. You may feel that these are strong words, and with this I will agree, for the words of truth always have a strength and clarity about them that can stir the emotions and stimulate insights.

For argument's sake, you may have examples in your repertoire that someone did do something explicit to you without your verbal permission. Maybe someone emotionally stabbed you in the back because of their deceitful impulses towards you, and you fully believe that you did not give them permission to hurt you.

Well, you did know deep down what was to happen and fully agreed to participate in the experience. The inner you helped set up the scenario so that you would have the opportunity to learn to react in an enlightened manner. You were a full participant on a specific level of interaction.

Back to our example of the chair-sitting seminar participant, if you are the one sitting in this chair, you agreed to listen to the speaker. After all, you travelled willingly to the venue from somewhere and probably paid a fair amount of money to get in the door, and you stayed sitting in the chair as the lecture progressed.

The next cleansing procedure probably needed another decision from you, this time a conscious decision to connect and agree with the procedure being offered. You are always in a constant state of decision-making of both conscious and subconscious choosing.

Now, it is one thing to choose something. The next step is to have this choice made known to both yourself and others, and to then set things in motion. A subconscious choice usually needs to make the conscious mind aware of it, so that viable actions are instigated.

For you to sit blankly in the chair while the practitioner does something or another shows to one and all that you have merely decided to sit in a chair. The practitioner may be busy attuning, adjusting things, prophesising, or even waving a magic wand over you, but none of these actions will hold or have any effect with you, unless you make a conscious decision to allow the effects to take root. So, in the end, it is you and you alone who decides to activate your inner resources to accept or deny whatever the practitioner is offering you.

To simply know is not to activate. To activate anything takes an input of your energy to set things in motion in any meaningful way. Even knowing facts and figures has its own movement and energy, but until you create a specific pattern about something, then set this pattern in motion to manifest in your physical world, they remain random and fairly jumbled movements.

I will suggest you think on this.

It is now a cool Sunday morning, with the sunshine peeking between the folds of the nearby hills and brushing the treetops in fresh and golden colours. The countryside is a beautiful and peaceful place right now, and all is well in my world.

Good morning, Samuel.

Good day, dearest daughter, a loving welcome to you. This will be a shorter session this morning.

Participation on a willing and conscious level is the tip of the iceberg. It is the unconscious decision-making that triggers most of your conscious choices, whether you consciously end up knowing this fact or not. You see, the way to become aware of your inner processes is to look at these inner workings in a deliberate way, whether this looking is through a quick moment of introspection or meditation practices, or however else you choose to monitor your gut instincts or intuitive impulses.

This action of activating your intuition and focusing your attention on the end results of the procedure needs to be done for you to be able to say that you consciously know what your unconscious mind is choosing and then manifesting for you.

That sentence is a mouthful, isn't it? You need to keep the conscious and unconscious understandings front and centre, because if you don't keep track you will find your thoughts tied in scrambled knots that give you a dose of indigestion, and you will spend time trying to work out where the unconscious trigger came from in the first place!

This is not really a hard action sequence to understand. You do it automatically many, many times a day by flicking back and forward between the internal layers of you, because it is a natural part of your cyclic nature.

If you are not aware of this internal movement of focus because of the movement and distractions of daily living, you will probably forget what you so fleetingly glanced at within your inner landscape. Of course, now and again you will get such a jolt of inner knowing that you do remember it in a more conscious way.

However, unless you have made the effort to train yourself into being always an aware and sensitive person, you will barely notice this constant shifting of attention between the inner and outer you. So, the more you can sense and connect with the inner you, the better you can understand what is involved in the full process of decision making, and in whether you will instigate any activity in a fuller and integrated way, and not just as a mildly interested bystander.

Liken what you're doing or instigating to a car, an auto-mobile that is sitting on its four round rubber tyres. It is just sitting there. Along comes a driver, and his name is Mr Focus. He opens the door and gets into the car, and he sits behind the wheel. This is setting the parameters of action, for a certain choice of activity to be selected, such as car-related activities like driving, tooting the horn, listening to the radio, swivelling the rear vision mirror, and so on.

When Mr Focus turns the key and starts the motor, this now becomes a field of action. The choice and preference of the possible action of driving has been selected. However, this is still only an indication of action choice because there has been enough mental and physical activity instigated to make this decision.

It was like the tip of an iceberg, seeing the possibilities for likely actions, but until the rest of the iceberg comes into play, the field is still limited to a specific field of action. It is when Mr Focus puts the car into gear and presses down firmly on the go pedal that the action of choice is being fully participated in.

Can you understand these distinctions between what I am describing? The actual difference between possible actions and physical actions?

Without the first concept or thought about driving being acted upon, the actual driving action would not have been successfully initiated. The tip of an iceberg is always connected to the larger underwater iceberg, so liken this underwater bit to the knowledge held within the subconscious mind.

This inner mind knew that Mr Focus needed to follow his destiny links. It knew he needed to be driving at this specific time, because he had the inner knowledge that he had to be somewhere specific soon, or he needed to be in a certain place to meet someone or do something important that Mr Focus maybe didn't consciously know about. There would always be reasons bubbling up from the depths that encourage everyone to follow destiny markers and actions. Mr Focus is no exception.

It is your physical movements that are the end result of a multi, lightning chain of electrical impulses, and it is the physical expression of these inner synapses that I would call the tip of the iceberg. All the hard work was done underneath.

So, now back to the car analogy.

Mr Focus could have stopped this chain of synapses from snapping and snarling quickly along the inner pathways at any time, but the action of driving the car would not have occurred. Mr Focus would not have been fully participating in the driving of the car, even though he was standing in the vicinity with the driving thought in mind.

Can you see the connection between this little car story and the story of the audience member participating in the seminar? Unless the action is fully carried through from first thought to complete manifestation, it is like the shattered iceberg that disperses and melts away into the surrounding water.

The experience of gardening has the same symbolic successes or failures. Say, for example, your inner processes may be nudging you from a corner of your mind, trying to make you aware that you have a soul need to get in touch with the natural world energy. Maybe you are very stressed out in some way and your inner doctor knows that this needs to be addressed in a healing way.

From deep within comes the rumbling thought or impression that you would love to grow some colourful poppies in your garden. You are not sure why you feel this need to grow poppies, but you go ahead and buy the seeds, prepare the soil, plant the seeds, water them, and tend to them carefully. You keep your focus on doing what is needed for these seeds to germinate and thrive, and in the fullness of time, blossom into the most magnificent flowers.

Any loss of continuity in the nurturing of these plants would more than likely result in dead or dying plants. The anticipated blooms would never spring into reality in your garden. Now, what you may not be consciously aware of and connected with is the fact that you needed the bright colours and the specific energy of the poppy flowers to help alleviate your stress.

At this point, I can almost hear the more colour-aware readers saying that this is a bad example, because red and bright orange colours have vibrations that increase physical strength and aliveness, and this may not be exactly what an overly stressed person would seem to need, one may think.

Well, if the person is stressed because of a deep physical tiredness, or a wobbly emotional energy wheel [chakra], the red, orange, or yellow would be extremely beneficial in boosting that general energy, and the clarity of the flower's colour would help bring much needed stability in the full body energetic system.

Of course there is more to this, because there is also the ambience of the garden work, the grounding of the stressful energies into the comforting warmth of Mother Earth, and so on, but to keep with the line of thought in this chapter, enough has been said.

The deeper and hidden end of the iceberg is your inner awareness doing what it can to bring the best possible choices for you into your conscious awareness. It is then up to you to decide whether you will participate or activate any of these choices.

Let me say here, it is not always easy to do what your inner promptings ask you to do. Your inner prompting is not a paid-up member of any local social union or club. It is not a family member who looks at you with big pleading eyes when asking you to do something.

Yet despite all the possible social difficulties that may arise, whatever the inner level of you actually needs and requests the outer you to do, it is always doable because you will never be asked to do the impossible.

There will always be a way to activate these inner world promptings in an outer world way. This may necessitate physical changes being made in how and where you are living; it may necessitate a lengthy preparation period. But these impulses, the true impulses from your Inner Self, are always reasonable and doable. If everything was easy, where would your challenges and your entertainment come from?

There is a great sense of fun and jollity around these words. As I initially write the words down, I try to put little smiley faces on the page, to remind me of the feelings that come through at any given time. There are two little smiley faces snuggled into the sentence at this point.

These smiley faces are great, but in truth when I read the words back, no matter how much time has gone by, I still feel and resonate with the wit and humour and all the feelings that came through originally.

Where would your stimulation come from? Alright, we know life isn't meant to be easy. Or is it? You decide. You decide whatever it is you are going to participate in, and it is you who decides if this participation will be using your full concentration and focus. It is you who will decide whether the ensuing result of any action will be classed as a successful action or not; or whether your participation will be as a wishy-washy bystander, and this interest will drift away into the great void.

Right, you have the picture. This I do tell you; in my many, many years, I have seen the wasted chances, the unused potential, the non-caring attitudes, the timidity, and the lack of self-confidence bring unhappiness and a desperate lack of fulfilment to so many, so many individuals.

Some people know the right action to take but are too lazy, too bombastic, too busy, and too overconfident to bring greatness into their lives. There will be a time of sadness when these souls eventually get to realise the opportunities they have lost, the wonderment and sense of fulfilment that they couldn't be bothered reaching out for.

Oh well. Another day, another time.

Or ... is there?

7

BODY PARTS —
PHYSICAL WOES AND WORRIES

G ood morning, dearest daughter. Would you like to talk
about your body parts now?

*Well, that was one of the best opening lines I have seen for a while.
There is a good chance there is going to be some interesting ideas come onto
the page this morning. I feel that this is going to be a fun book session,
simply because of that question. A fun session, with maybe some hard
truths to digest.*

Do you regularly go to your local doctor to get pills to help
ease your physical aches and pains? Do you put up with lame-
ness or headaches simply because it is deemed to be a part of
growing old, or a result of the type of life you lead? Do you
expect to lose your memory as you add more earth years onto
your current cycle?

Do you expect this or that to happen to you, just because
it is written in the medical journals that this or that always happens to people when they reach a certain age? Are you fully
committed to keeping this progressive degeneration going on
in your physical body, as per a schedule that someone else has
put onto a written form?

Do you feel that you look older than other people of similar years, or do you feel that you look younger than your peers? All this is quite an interesting subject, isn't it?

Each person has his or her own specific ideas about physical health and how to develop a healthy lifestyle, or they have many reasons not to think about their health and don't want to be bothered by it at all.

Everyone who is interested has many personal opinions that range from interested but wanting to keep everything simplistic, to being dedicated to learning about health and studying detailed and specific areas of interest.

Countless words have been written and read on the topic of how to remain healthy. There are so many books and articles written and published in the public media about this subject of healthy living. A reader cannot miss being bombarded with information about someone's hobby horse on certain health issues.

This information is out in the public arena; in fact, there is too much information, and what is even worse is much of the information being offered contains conflicting advice and theories. Therefore, I put it to you, the informed and concerned reader, what are you meant to believe?

How does one go about logically finding out who is speaking truth and who is not? And why is this subject of physical health being spoken about in a book like this one, one that is mainly writing about the non-physical things in life?

Well, while you are wrapped in your physical coat on this turn of the wheel, you can't not be aware of, and concerned about, your physical bits and pieces. There is no separation between your skin and the inner Spark that animates you.

This loving and caring of all parts of your creative expression means that you need to love, cherish, and nurture your physical bits and pieces as well as the non-physical bits. That's logical. Let it be put simply: to love, nurture, and care for your physical self is a physical expression of your Inner Soul's caring nature.

You are expressing your inner energy in a visible way, so you can see outwardly [with your physical eyes] the inner expressions. And despite that sentence being a curly one, it too is logical in its makeup.

Does this sound familiar?

Yes, of course it does. The same actions, the same energy paths, are being used to bring into manifestation your inner choices. Ah ha! See, here is that word 'choice' again. This time you are intimately connected in every way to the ensuing result of these inner decisions; you actually carry these results around with you like a turtle that carries its house of shell.

So, too, do you carry your inner house of choices in your physical shell. There is no singular place to store one set of decisions, and no other place to store another set of decisions, because there is no separation of anything, anywhere and anytime.

Can you hear the chuckle that Samuel is trying to hold back? Right now, there is a strong sense of jollity and a sense of the ridiculous that Samuel is emitting as he dictates, because he has talked, time and time again, in different ways, about there being no separation of anything. And here he has used another example of this.

Everyone can see the results of your inner beliefs and the choices that spring into reality from these beliefs you hold about yourself. Well, the issue to think about is this: are you fully satisfied with the body you are living in and walking around in? Or are you dissatisfied with only a small part of this body?

Are you totally unhappy about your height, your weight, race, skin colour, nose, chin, hair, or any other aspects that come to mind? Have you got bits and pieces that you would change in a heartbeat, if you had the ability to do so? Hmm, hmm?

This is not going to be a chapter on how to keep healthy as per diet and lifestyle choices. There is enough information out there to help you make valid and informative choices about courses of actions. I give you some other ideas on this subject of health to think on, ideas that may come from an angle you may not have thought about at all.

The body that has been surgically changed to make the wearer feel he or she is conforming to society's standard of beauty does not hide the inner character of the person who wears this body. In fact, it brings any uncertainties, lack of self-confidence, fears, and foibles out into the open for everyone to see even more clearly. For example, usually non-life changing cosmetic [beauty surgery] is a camouflaging action. So, who is trying to fool who?

Be honest about why your body is looking and acting as it is. Do you truly look after it in a caring, intelligent, and nourishing way? Do you pamper it with expensive cosmetics, yet forget to feed it enough protein? Do you ensure a balanced nurturing?

Look around you. Look at the people in your locality, and see the different shapes, sizes, and packages that bodies come in. It is indeed variable and unlimited. If you do this while looking at others with your inner eye, you will see immediately what the targeted person thinks about themself.

Do you see a muscle builder flaunting his muscles before everyone whose attention he can grab? Is he building up muscle to build up the inner confidence he is lacking, or is he so in love with his own being, he desires to concentrate all his attention on himself? Is this one an egotist? Or a scaredy cat?

Just having a quick, intuitive glance at different people will give you a good reading on their inner characters. For the readers who will now point out to me that many people hide themselves in pretentious activity, in camouflaging their actions, and in physical playacting, let me tell you straight.

Yes, there are many people doing this camouflaging, but it does not matter what they have attempted. Because everyone's working intuition will see under the camouflage people have created and know who and what they are and will hone into their truth. The truth of the person.

People, there is no successful way of hiding behind physical props, behind expensive clothes, cosmetic surgeries, fancy homes, and picture-book-pretty living spaces, or even the reverse of a plentiful and a positive lifestyle. If you are one of the souls who tries to deliberately hide their personal issues and true self from others, it does not matter what you do. Those with the intuitive ability to sense things around corners, and with the eyes to see, will see beneath the coverings and read what is in your heart. Always. The previous chapter had some further comments about this.

On a more personal note, if you are unsatisfied with an aspect of your physical body, go deep within [meditate!] and find out why you have chosen to be like you are at the moment. You may find deep insecurities wanting to be soothed.

You may find, as an example, that your crippled leg is meant to slow you in some manner, so you have more 'time' to do what is needed in your best interests. Maybe it is meant to stop you rushing around senselessly as you did in a previous life experience.

Or if you are small, you may find that your short physical stature has been pre-planned by you, for you to be put in the position where you need to be able to deal with physical lifestyle frustrations, a life where you just cannot reach out and grab what you want to grab.

Or you may find that your excess weight is being used as a shield to keep people away from you until you are more confident and surer about your ability to withstand perceived emotional hurts.

You may have eye problems that force you to look innerwards instead of outerwards during this lifetime. And so on, and so on, examples infinitum!

It is having a deeper understanding that there actually is a reason why you have chosen how you look physically. It is the understanding that there are specific reasons or a major overriding reason why you have chosen to express this in a specific physical way. And it is the understanding that you can alter either partly or fully, the physical or outer manifestation of this inner belief that makes life on this Planet so valuable and exciting.

The simple fact is that if you acknowledge that you are responsible for how you act and how you look, this powerfully changes everything about your self-expression. You begin to sense the personal power and decision-making coming back to you, because it slowly begins to flow back to you from health practitioners, health and beauty experts, and from everyone else.

The power to change is the most formidable of powers, and you deserve to control your destiny in this area. I am not saying to throw away all help and medical advice; far from it.

I am saying to use your intuition and be flexible, and to allow yourself to have a say in what happens to your health history.

A good way to empower the way of expressing yourself is this: change your inner belief, and the physical will follow. Again, I can hear the detractors shouting, "What about the people who have lost a limb, what do they do?" Well, in such a case, when the deeper understanding of why they lost the limb hits home, a new attitude will emerge. The limb will not grow back, but there will be such a change in attitude that any change becomes a life-enhancing change.

Maybe the amputee will stop feeling so victimised and will go to the trouble of getting a prothesis [or not], then get out and about with a cheerful attitude and help other amputees understand their situation from a new and enriching angle. Maybe the insight will bring a new thought into conscious awareness that, when explored fully, results in a new and more exciting career coming into reality. There are unlimited ways to express this new understanding of why you are as you physically are.

Do you always feel unwell? Then meditate on this and find the trail that leads you to insightful answers. You know that illness is not something that you catch, or something that you pick up from another person – because you know that even a contagious influenza epidemic will leave some people from among the many untouched.

If you expect to catch the influenza virus because the health authorities are telling you that you are in the category of people who are at risk of catching it, then catch it you will. Look closely at the word catching. It is a doing word, a doing by you. You catch you.

If you put out your hands and obediently catch the influenza virus, then you have done it for a reason, and it was done for you to have that physical experience, an inner need or belief that wanted to come forth from the depths within. It all ends up, again, as your personal choice to experience the influenza.

A new day begins, and it is another rainy morning. It has been raining gently since yesterday. The little green frogs have come out of their hiding places and are clinging to the wall around the patio door and on the rafters. They are enjoying the experience. It is a bountiful time for the native citizens of the local woods.

It is rather pleasant to be seated at the table, with a pen and paper at the ready, a candle lit as a symbolic Light source, the beautiful spider webs glistening with the light drops of rain that cling to the strands. I feel at home amongst the beautiful countryside.

So, we begin to see under the reasons why you may have physical health problems. What you have to contend with in this field is the fact that there is not always an obvious physical cause for you to quickly latch onto. The health correction procedures need to be started in the energetic side of things.

This might seem like nonsense to many people, especially those who do not believe there is more to the body than what can be seen. Meanwhile, the people who know that the Spirit is supreme will understand fully the insights that have just been expressed.

Where do you fit in all this? Have you thought about your physical woes in any other way than *it's expected at my age*, or *the doctor told me it was normal stresses and lifestyle reactions?* And do you feel you are a victim of someone or something? And so on, examples unlimited.

You have accepted these reasons and do not look elsewhere for the answers.

As I was writing the above down, I had the strongest urge to also put down the schoolkids' excuse of 'The dog ate my homework'. I suppose that excuse is as valid as any other.

I do strongly suggest that you open your mind and look further for the answers if you are stuck in any of the above-mentioned ruts. The answers and solutions lie elsewhere. This elsewhere is not any long distance away, and you do not have to go into panic mode when you thinking about the impracticalities of organising a worldwide travel itinerary. The journey you need to make is much shorter, more powerful, and more essential to the understanding of any physical issues than any other action you may take.

Meditate.

And to meditate means to journey within.

There has been quite a lot written about meditation: how to do it, how not to do it, and all the nuts and bolts of the practice. If you have never meditated, make the effort to find someone to show you how, go join a class, read the appropriate books. Just decide, then do it.

The action of doing a regular meditation session will change your life in many ways. As you learn your own individual techniques and patterning, you will be able to go out travelling the inner and outer landscapes in the quest for answers to questions about your physical aspects. This is the best advice that anyone can give you on this subject.

As you meditate you relax your physical stresses, so immediately your body will respond in a positive and powerful way. This is a double-edged benefit and one that everyone needs to take advantage of.

For those busy people who say that they do not have the 10 or 30 minutes a day for mediation, I say this to them: what are you afraid of? Why do you keep yourself so insanely busy that you do not give yourself time to see you as you really are? A veneer of 'busyness' is an effective camouflage shielding, but it doesn't fool anyone other than you.

Right, here is the deal. You make your own reality; this is known to be an undisputed fact. If you are unhappy about any situation or physical expression about yourself, then change it … or at the very least, alter your perceptions of it!

Do it. Change it. Believe it.

8

LOVE IS THE KEY

L ove is the key, the key to all things, and this cannot be said enough times. I am not speaking about the gushy romantic love that two people will share whilst in the full blossoming of a new physical romance.

The love I speak of is a feeling of total togetherness, of rightness and of belonging, the feeling of being at peace with all things. This love is the knowledge of a connection so profound that it just IS. You feel it in your bones, and in your heart, in such a profound way that the physical expression of it is secondary.

True love does not need to be demonstrated in any way, because the people involved know it is there so deeply within, that any surface demonstrations are superfluous. True love flows from your heartbeat and from each and every breath you take. True love radiates from your inner core and ripples out, unstoppable from there.

When you are truly in the 'state of grace', your inner aspects change in many ways and these changes can be felt by even the densest and less enlightened of people because you will radiate strength and such a feeling of calmness and control, your 'state of grace' becomes obvious to all.

Also, this inner state changes the way you react to outside stimuli. For example, if someone is leaning very close to you and shouting obscenities with much energy and venom right into your face, your own inner strength of love allows you to become a transformer of this angrily expressed energy.

You do not take the words into your heart, but instead the quiet and loving strength within you sallies forth into the angry one's spaces and gently begins to transmute the hurtful passion broiling within them. The abusive shouter slowly winds down their tirade because he or she realises that none of the abuse is hitting the target. You have become a non-stick target.

This beautiful and loving strength allows you to go through life, not as a will-o'-the-wisp that is being tossed around by every little erratic wind current that happens by. Not exactly as a bystander either, but more as an interested participant who becomes unattached to any of the outcomes, as one who is strong within their own space, and also as someone who will always emanate a loving and calming influence that helps other people around them draw on this freely given strength and clarity.

The true loving energy allows you to live in a way of such connectiveness and togetherness with all living things because it sets new parameters for how you react to people and events of all kinds. You see things differently, you know things in a more simple and basic way, and it is a beautiful and a continually empowering way to live your life.

The inner state of love and strength acts as a pillar within that supports you at all times. This inner pillar lives in and comes from the heart of you, the core, the centre of your Being. And it is this centre that not only stabilises you in your physical reality but is the doorway into all other realities about you.

As you travel through these other realities, this strength of love, this pillar of 'you' becomes the anchor from which you venture forth. Yes, you have been told many times, in many sermons, books, and lectures, to love yourself and your fellow humans, yet many of these sources do not truly explain what this love is, and how to get 'it' programmed into your system.

Well, this I can tell you; the total **love of all things** I am talking about is **already programmed** into your cellular matrix. All you need to do is go to the trouble of expending some energy and uncovering it, so that it can work with full and expressive efficiency. You always have had this love within you; you have never been without it. How about that for an efficient situation?

There is a lovely feeling of gentle humour and magnanimity being expressed by Samuel here, and I am getting a dose of what is possible to feel as the warm and fuzzy love motes gently wash over absolutely every-thing in existence. This is a magical moment, and right now, all is well in my world.

Physical love is just the smallest expression of the pro-found and total "life love" that I am speaking of. Physical love is, at best, a transitory showing of deep inner emotions, and it is a wonderful and extremely enjoyable experience that every-one needs to experience at one time or another.

The love I keep talking about is the deep connection that drives the physical expressions. This deep love carries on regardless of whether there is physical contact or not. This contact is an active energy contact from the core heart to the core heart, and there is no physical activity that can shatter this linkage.

No physical betrayal of one person or the other in any given relationship will make a dent in the true solidity of this inner connection. Do you understand where I am going with this?

True Love of All Things empowers you in a way so profound that miracles seem to be the norm, and you are never caught out because no matter what happens to you, you identify with the happening in a total and committed way. You walk around with such strength and solidness that nothing can knock you off your feet.

You and you, and yes, even you, can uncover this godly Love of All Things that is in your cellular matrix. Little snippets will have been escaping from their inner hiding places at various times in your life, but you need to uncover the full range and strength of this love.

Take the lid off. Open the door. Let the light flood within and rummage in the attic of your heart. See if you can take the bindings off the most precious parcel of all. All you need is the desire and intent to do this.

All you need is to expend the energy on the knowledge that this magical parcel is there for you to find, and to allow the removal of all restrictions, with the intention of allowing the Loving God Within free and full reign in your life. It excites me just to write about it all.

There is a wonderful sense of expectation, of joyful curiosity and maybe some impatience coming through with these words. I can 'see' Samuel's eyes shining brightly with excitement and loving energy.

Right from the beginning of this morning's session, the words have been pouring out gleefully and quickly onto the page, and it has been a challenge to keep up with the pace and still make the writing sort of legible.

Funny thing, even though I am writing this comment myself, the energy is still strong and I can barely keep up with my own words. It is rather a lovely feeling to have such beautiful energy to work with.

Look around you. You will see some people who have achieved a certain degree of this inner calmness and loving strength of which I speak, and as you look, you will also note how these people draw others to their radiant strength, into their loving energy. They are like magnets.

The people around them cannot get enough of this freely given and loving presence. Do your own research on this; it will not take you long to see the shining ones amongst the populace because they are the ones who stand apart from others in the crowd.

Do you want to be like these shining ones? You can be. I give you permission for you to give you permission to be so. How about that for word convolution? But do reread it for the jest that it is. I can give you permission to do anything, but even I know it is an invalid permission. It is you and you only who can give you permission to do anything.

I have spoken of this in another context, but now you know it does not matter what the context or situation is; only you have the power to move the mountains within.

Your choice to be ... or not to be.

Your choice to do ... or not to do.

Your choice to love ... or not to love.

Ad infinitum.

Manifesting this inner pillar of strength comes from the decision to activate the search for your spiritual nature and explore all the ramifications that flow from this search. You will need to become a Warrior of Light, as I, among the many, call the seeking ones, and to continue on this path by dealing with and understanding all of life's lessons that come into your personal orbit, the lessons and situations that you know you need to deal with.

It is an intelligent and intuitive journey that begins with the uncovering of the magical parcel labelled Love that is to be found always in the internal pillar of the heart. As you work your way through the lessons, layer by layer, the unwrapping or covering is taken from the parcel. Usually this is a gradual process, more so than a heart-stopping moment of insight, and it entails a steady progress of delving within to ensure a successful outcome.

So, here is the situation. Do you honestly feel that you have such an inner strength of heart, the Love of All Things, that you can handle anything that life throws at you?

You do not have to be a stoic, a person who reacts to very little. Indeed, the expressing of emotions is a wonderful release, and this releasing is a part of your inherent makeup. Do you feel the inner pillar of strength so strongly that you are able to access it at any time you need to?

Do you feel that you are able to step aside even briefly, for a moment, even in the direst of circumstances, and at that time, see the bigger picture that is unfolding before you? And only then make the choice of action that this bigger picture calls for you to make? Despite this call being different to what your conscious mind is screaming at you to do?

It is the time when you are under pressure that the inner Pillar of Love and Strength needs to be communicated with and worked with in a direct and limitless way.

When this inner strength is there, it changes how you react. For instance, you may feel that Ahale holds me [Samuel the Prophet] in a specially enshrined place, a place that is kept just for visiting Angels, High Spirits, Gods and Goddesses, indeed, a special place of awe and wonder.

Yet talk to her and she will describe me as a friendly old uncle. This is the truth; she has explained her feelings about me thusly in many instances. There is a connection between us that does not allow idol worshipping to enter the fray.

This is how it all could be and, in fact, really is. There is a feeling of completeness, of being at one, at home, with all living things. There is no feeling that I am holier than she is. All is one, and one is all, and this is a very tangible state between us both.

Ahale and I come together now because in a pre-birth [Ahale's] planning session, we decided to do these writings. So, there is a strong sense of the familiar for her. This is not seen or felt to be an alien or an extraordinary contact in any way, but it seems and feels to be a normal one.

By the way, Ahale took some of her allotted lifetime – in fact, decades – to reach this point of remembering. She took some strong shaking up to even begin the true search for her memories, and she had even forgotten the name that we had agreed to use for this bookwork.

Oh, I didn't think Samuel was going to say anything personal about me like that. It is true though what he is saying, because it took some major life traumas to get me shuffling forward into regular meditative practices, which resulted in me having to negotiate many very steep learning curves. There are enough anecdotal experiences readily available for another book.

There are many such authors who are co-authoring spirit books, many who feel similar emotional connections to the spiritual contacts such as Ahale is going through. There is this loving connection that takes away all the strangeness, the other worldliness from these spirit contacts, and this makes all contact seem totally normal.

Of course it is. Because all these channelling authors are working with spirit friends they have worked with before, and they have all known each other since time began. So, a loving heart does bring a new perspective to the ones who have strengthened this inner loving light. Actually, a truer description would be that this is more of a renewal of remembrance of previous activities.

And with the last word, the energy of Samuel was quickly gone. I still held the pen in my hand, ready to continue writing, but that indeed proved to be the end of the session.

To me it was an extraordinary dictation. The energy coming through was riveting and electric, and when it was gone, there was a real feeling of emptiness. It was also a longer than usual session.

9

YOU ARE THE STRANGER —
COSMIC SURGERY

8 a.m. Good morning, dearest readers, and how are you all this fine day? Do you have a wonderful day planned out already? Or are you dreading even the thought of having to go to a boring job, or cleaning the house, making sandwiches for the never-ending school lunches, or any mundane tasks, ad infinitum?

"Oh … woe is me! I have to do all these uninteresting tasks. Why do I have to do them? Why cannot someone else do them? Oh … boo hoo!"

You poor dear. If you are thinking along these lines, it really is a double "boo hoo", because, as you now know, you are not only you, but you are also everybody else. You have remembered this, have you not?

Right now, you cannot escape the essential you and the life situations that you find yourself in. This is a simple fact. However, you also now know that you can begin to change how you perceive your current situation, and you can now see it for the most magnificent and inspiring setup on learning how to deal successfully with all events, and all emotional output.

In fact, whatever it is that you have decided to learn as you go through this lifetime on the most beautiful planet you call Home, you can change your circumstances. You can do this by simply stepping aside from the position you are now looking at everything from. Just take a big step to one side, out into another position, and look back at your life from another aspect, another angle.

This instantly changes your humdrum existence and usually does so in interesting ways. You may well surprise yourself at what this new angle, this new viewpoint, brings out of the shadows and into the light.

Imagine that you are the stranger [to you]; a stranger who is non-judgemental, is fair in all dealings, is kind and emanates loving energy from the heart at all times. This stranger is looking at you, your place of living, your family or lack of family, and your total lifestyle situation. This stranger can see into your heart, can see your strengths and perceived weaknesses.

This stranger can see your potential and how much of this potential you are currently activating. This stranger is honest and is well able to see into everything, even the bits and pieces you would like to stay hidden.

Now, in the 'I am the stranger' guise, look back at the real you and assess what you are seeing. You will be pleasantly surprised, because all the social impositions and expectations that overlay your 'you-ness' will have been stripped away or fully peeled aside so the true you can be revealed.

It is now possible for a much clearer picture to be seen.

Even though you may be living in dire poverty with all the nitty gritty problems that scenario entails, or you are living within restrictions of some kind, you [as the stranger looking at the real you] may note a strong and quiet strength of persistence and survival that overlays everything you are doing as you go about the daily grind.

The stranger may see a 'preparedness for action' being built up, and a readiness to meet whatever life throws at you. This viewer may note how your generous heart opens wide to give compassionate and emotional support to others in their hours of need.

Many such nobilities of the spirit will be more readily seen when you look from different angles and with the fresher eyes of an interested watcher.

On the other side of the coin, this stranger that is you will be able to see more clearly why you have allowed yourself and your emotions to maybe feel negative and uninspired. The blanket of gloom and boredom will be seen in situ, but what is of interest here, the doorway that leads to the removal of these negative aspects, will be shown.

You, as the stranger, will see more of the opportunities that are always around you. You will see more of the linked and chained connections that when grasped firmly in hand will guide you out of the doldrums and into a refreshing new life. Your living circumstances may not change in any immediate way, but the way you look at these circumstances most certainly will.

Do not despair if you are living in untenable circumstances and cannot see any way out of the trap you feel you are in. Despair only keeps you from seeing the opportunities and possibilities that are out there and within reach of your questing hand. You live in a bubble of opportunity whether you can see this bubble or not.

If you own a television set and the picture suddenly disappears, you will probably check to make sure all the electrical connections are still good, or you will look to see if the pet dog has perhaps pulled the power cord out of the wall socket during a playful romp. You will keep looking until you have found the source of the problem, and then you will fix it.

Take this analogy and place it over your own hiccups or issues. You need to keep looking at every aspect you can think of, until you find why you are having the problems you are having. Keep at this exercise until you understand. Tweak and twist the inner focus into all the nooks and crannies within, until you find a picture that is being presented in a clearer and understandable format.

Your life is never hopeless at any time. There are always wonderful, unusual, and stimulating alternate situations for you to focus on. Even if you are not needy in the monetary arena, you may feel that life has treated you badly in some other way.

Maybe you cannot find true love despite trying hard to find it; maybe your family does not want to visit you; maybe your health is not very robust; maybe the tax man is not dealing fairly with you.

Hey there!

Life is not treating you badly at all; it is you who is treating life badly.

Did you note the words just written? You create your own circumstances, so as the builder of these circumstances, you have within you the power and the knowledge to alter, rebuild, pull down, and transform these circumstances in any way your Spirit leads you.

Note well that I say 'Spirit leads'; so never confuse this with what your emotions 'want' or your conscious mind 'wants'. The change needs to come from your inner instincts, otherwise, any changing or renovating will just be a reshuffling of old issues and styles. You will not be altering your circumstances in ways that will lead you to find the golden door of enlightenment.

Even if you feel locked into any life situation, do the "I am a stranger looking back at me" exercise. See what nuances there are, and how many chinks in the wall around that you can see, because there is light even in the darkest of corners, and this is something that you always need to remember.

In fact, when this is acknowledged, the joyful eruption of this light into freedom and expansion can be breathtaking and profound. Give the light an inch and it will take a mile. Give the light an open chink in a wall to flow through, and it will gleefully widen this gap so that the breach is as wide as it can be made.

Do you love the way it all comes together, a time when everything begins flowing smoothly? That is how it is all meant to be.

Unfortunately, it is an uncommon state of affairs, especially with anyone who has the stresses of daily life leaning heavily on their shoulders. Make a conscious decision today and decide that you will become aware of all opportunities towards enlightened change that you can.

And what is more important, decide to do something positive with these chances that are being presented to you. These may be both large and small opportunities. It does not matter the size of the action. Just connect into the chance in a positive manner.

At the end of the day, recap what has been noted and subsequently activated. Did you become even more despairing because you could not see any opportunities to do anything new? Did you pick up on something, but decided not to go ahead with it because it would have made you look silly?

Or did you take the chance to take the leap of faith from the clifftop, the leap that took you out of the entrenched rut you were in, a leap that enabled you to take the chance and leap into a new idea, friendship, or opportunity?

Look into your heart and make an honest assessment as to whether you can be bothered to go to any effort at all to improve not only your physical circumstances but your emotional and spiritual stability.

Too many people lose the chance of great enlightenment because they couldn't be bothered; their excuses for not putting any personal effort into any introspection and action may be trite.

The effort involved may have been to meditate for ten minutes instead of watching a favourite television show, or it may have necessitated getting out of bed half an hour earlier each day, so you had a quiet and peaceful time for yourself to read your wisdom books yet still allowed time to finish all the daily chores.

There will be truckloads of reasons the reluctant person will be able to think of to do nothing, and so by using any reason, they sabotage their ability to become a great beacon of light among the multitudes.

Strange, isn't it? Some people are envious of successful people and want what they have, but not often will you find these envious ones are prepared to put out the physical, mental, and emotional effort that is required to achieve similar success. An interesting quirk in the field of human idiosyncrasies.

Ah well, the same level of successful would never have eventuated anyway, because if someone does put out energy and application, and does try to emulate a successful person, this endeavour will probably be successful, but it will not be as a clone of the other. The success will emerge into reality in a personal way and never as a clone of anybody else.

Mirror, mirror on the wall …

The mirror throws back your image, not anyone else's. Whatever you do, change, or fiddle with, the result is being done to you.

You may change your hairstyle because you like the way this style looks on one of your role models. You may save up the needed money, go to the hairdresser, and have your hair styled in an identical way as worn by your hero/heroine. You then go home and look in the mirror and decide you are satisfied with your hairdo. Now, take a step back from your image and ask yourself these questions:

Do I feel more successful now I have a beautiful haircut that looks like my favourite television actor's hair?

Will this action change my life for the better?

Does this hairstyle really suit me, and does it help bring out my personality?

Am I trying to be someone that I am not?

Am I trying to latch on to someone else's success?

And so forth.

You will still be you, just with someone else's hair styling. You see, it is your heart and soul that determines who you are, not a hairstyle. So please be honest about why you feel the need to copy another person's characteristic appearance, be it facial features being changed with cosmetic surgery, hairstyle, clothing, or behavioural patterns.

Can you make the effort to see what suits you and your personality best? Can you make the effort to go into each new day with a light and loving heart and deal insightfully with each and every situation that comes your way?

As you awaken each day, can you look at this new day as a day of supreme opportunity and joyful tasks, no matter how menial these tasks feel to you at the time? Can you make a sandwich for someone you may not like, in an open-hearted and loving way? Can you? You don't want to, even if you can?

Can the can, and open the box
Take out the love, it's deep in the socks
Of footwear you keep, so clean in the drawer
Take out the love, let it become aired
Shake out the blues, let love become shared

I have always said that I am not a poet, but I do so love these 3-second little ditties. Hey there, dear reader, I feel you are maybe also good at doing these fun jingles. Why not pick up a pen and do three quick little ditties on some aspect of your day-to-day living?

It may surprise you what comes flowing out from your mind.

Give it a go. Be spontaneous and do your own rhyming, because it is almost certain to be better than mine, and do you know, it would not worry me in the least if it was better. Not all angels have a poetic nature, and we all have our different strengths and not-so-strong strengths [never weaknesses].

Alright, in this chapter I have asked you some wide-ranging and in-depth questions, for example:

Why do you want to wear your hair like everyone else's?

Do you happily give food to others?

Will you write out a fun ditty?

These all may seem like stupid little questions to you at first reading, but each answer you honestly give will bring you great insights into how and whether the inner you is being deliberately blindfolded by the outer you; and whether you are actually communicating with this inner you.

These everyday activities show that even the most mundane daily activity has merit and is worth doing well and with loving intent. They all do count. They are important in a most profound way.

Your Spiritual expression comes through for everyone to see, with each breath that you take, with each small gesture, with each task you do, in your general manner and intent in each and every action you physically do or even think about.

If this concept frightens you just a little bit, then look closely and see exactly what you are thinking about as you do anything. Are you grumbling about 'something' and always thinking negative thoughts that ensure you will draw and attract into your life more of the same? Or will you see that even the most unglamorous chore has a godliness of action imbued within it?

Have you thought about your ditty yet? I will be watching and listening.

Yes, this is the end of this chapter. Go out and take your photo.

That last comment was in response to a thought that had just flashed through my mind. I had glanced up and seen a huge spider's web glistening in the morning light. It was not far from the window that I look out of when I am sitting at the table I use as my desk.

A ray of the early morning sun lit up the web in a golden and silvery light. I wanted to go and immediately take a photograph of it.

I did rustle around, got out the camera, climbed through the fence, and scuttled among the loose rocks, but by the time I got within a good picture-taking distance, the ray of sunlight had moved just enough to bring the shadow over half of the huge web. I took the photo anyway and it actually turned out better than I expected. So much for my negative thoughts.

There was a lot of good humour coming from Samuel during this session. I am not sure how this humour is best described, especially when he goes into simple yet convoluted word play that seems to have hidden depths. All I can do is make a note of what I feel and leave it at that for now.

10

WHAT IS REAL?
THE RISING HEARTBEAT

"Love makes the world go around."

You have all heard this adage in one language or another. Do you feel it is the truth?

Well, of course it is. Love is the energy of the Creative Force, so it is the muscle that glues all realities together. Why do some people feel so unloved when they live in a cosmic soup made of loving energy? Would you agree that this may be because they do not understand they are actually a living part of a huge and unlimited bundle of love?

Love has no boundaries. There are no fences between your reality and all other realities, yet many people, including some of the sensitive ones, will tell you they see symbolic boundaries of sorts between realities.

Now, the question that needs to be asked is this: Why do they feel the need to see boundaries, or limiting lines of awareness? Is it so they don't have to confront the wide-open big picture, a big picture that includes unknowns like ghosts and goblins, angels and devils, and even flying saucers with their little green men inside?

Fun images are floating and moving rapidly across the ticker tape area of my visionary arena. Little green aliens? Why green and not orange aliens? And now these strange little ones are rushing around and arguing about their colours.

Anyone who has conscientiously meditated in an effective way will tell you that, as they become more efficient in letting go all conscious control, they find themselves visiting some very alien, weird, and wonderful worlds where they meet up with star people, space men, monsters, and maidens. Whatever, and whoever resides in these wonderful worlds are the uncountable many.

Some people who meditate will also tell you that these weird and wonderful aliens communicated with them in such a way that they came out of their meditation with new insights, and new thoughts and feelings about their life situations that eventually proved to be very beneficial and life enhancing.

So, where do these alien and strange places emerge from? Are they all fragments of the meditating person's imagination? Are they real in the sense they have a physical body? Or are they nebulous figments of someone else's imagination coming to deliberately scare the meditator?

Well, yes and no to the last question.

Let us work through an example. Say, for instance, your meditating friend was trying hard in all ways to stay on his or her Path of Light, and during each meditation was asking for any helpful advice to be given to him/her by the respective Guardian Angels. This is a fairly normal practice, to set up an intent before one begins to meditate. That is, the meditator has the intent to focus on receiving an answer to a specific question or insights into a specific situation.

Let us say that the meditator asks for help in determining the next thing, issue, book, or activity that he or she needs to do. Yet as this person sinks deeper and deeper into a self-induced trance state, he or she finds themselves being whisked and whooshed through solid rock, flowing and swimming through the rock molecules, then coming out into a beautiful green valley in a world that sort of looks like Mother Earth, but in fact could be just about anywhere.

While the meditator is resting on a rock in this valley, a human-like figure approaches them where they sit on the warm rock, wondering what is to happen next.

This approaching figure is clothed in leather vest and leggings, with a marvellous feathered headdress and beaded and feathered wrist and anklet bands. This Being does not speak, but from Its presence emanates the most wonderful feeling of love and of strength.

As this Star Being smiles at the one sitting on the rock, he/she receives the strongest and most intense feeling that they have come HOME. It is a very emotional moment and the feelings are profound.

The Star Being takes from his vest a golden key and silently offers it to the rock-sitting one, who reaches out and takes it, holding it reverently in his or her hands. In a flash of shimmering light, the Star Being disappears. The meditator turns and retraces the journey through the rock, again flowing or swimming through the rock, with the golden key clasped firmly to their chest.

Now, when the meditation is over, everything is remembered as clearly and in as explicit detail as the tone of a well-tuned bell.

What do you feel has happened during this meditation, dear readers? Was it all just a flight of a vivid imagination? Well, simply this, the meditating person actually went travelling. Their Inner Spirit sent out a splinter of their Core Energy, and this energy splinter travelled the vast, yet no, distance into other realities.

This meditation was a true travel experience, and the travelling 'splinter of focus' energy became as an envoy for the person who was sitting in the chair meditating. The messenger was sent out to receive, retrieve, and return with the information that had been requested at the beginning of the meditation.

The Star Being also was real, in fact, more real in the true sense than the physical meditator. This Star Being came from the place that is HOME, the place where the meditator **first knew, and first remembered** he or she was indeed a part of the Great Creation. This Home place differs with people, because one Star System may feel like home to some people more so than it does to others.

The golden key was a part of the message that was sent from the home Cosmos Energy gestalt. The key means that a golden opportunity is to come into the life of the meditator. This will necessitate using their spiritual skills [key] to access and successfully implement whatever needs to be implemented.

The message implied loud and clear that the seeker was on the correct and rightful path to continue the process of enlightenment. This example is based on a true meditation, and there is more to this story, but the outline is enough to set the scene for this illustration.

Many people have unstructured journeys during meditation. That does not mean that the meditation is an invalid one.

If you can rule out the presence of too much alcohol, the taking of mind-altering drugs, or too much food being eaten during the last meal taken, the meditation will be a valid one.

A fractured meditation is showing the meditator that some fracturing is being reflected from their personal lives into the meditation ritual. Yet even here, there will be valid clues. Real messages, real journeying, all hidden between the fragments.

Each fractured fragment has validity, and these types of journeys need to be looked at both in piecemeal and as a whole, because many messages and places of interest may have been quickly visited, but little hints and clues will have been picked up here and there.

Maybe many different realities were quickly visited, sort of like a child rushing around on a treasure hunt in Grandmama's back garden, taking a rushed peek here and a quick look there. Many realities may have been quickly visited in the rushed quest for insights and information.

All these quickly scanned realities are valid places in their own right, and it is this fact that makes sense of some meditations and dreams. This reality travel is a ticklish and alien concept for many people to believe in. Well, we can only keep repeating the fact. You are more than just a person who walks around covered in a physical coat.

You have **been** since time began. You are a Child of the Universe. You are a Galactic Citizen. You have lived in distant galaxies. You have lived with and known well the Starmen and the Starwomen, like the one who came to visit in the previous meditation illustration.

You, as you are now, are a most magnificent Soul, a soul who has the vast knowledge of the Space Lanes, and the spiderweb of the Galactic Connections. You know of the vastness of the time scale, the scale that can never be put into a true measurement of time as you know it to be in your tick-tock time. You know these other realities are real because you have journeyed amongst them since time began.

So, please do not throw away meditation or dream experiences just because you deem them unreal or too weird. You have been amongst the weird and wonderful. You have many weird and wonderful friends out there in what you may believe to be alien worlds.

Please remember, I am not just talking about the solid planets and star systems that you see with your wonderful telescopes. These are, of course, included in the whole, but they are only one visible spectrum of a huge and unlimited Creation.

There are worlds within worlds, realities within realities. There are no fences; there are no boundaries. It is all a matter of different energy vibrational frequencies, and how good or insightful enough you are at any time to be able to see and visit within these vibrational levels.

Right now, you have chosen to explore a certain group of vibrational worlds; hence, your physical nature and the personal placement in this physically manipulating world. You can travel easily within a certain radius from where you are, yet further travelling can also be done easily when you change your travel mode.

Your vibrational energy 'messenger focus' can travel many worlds, and through many vibrational whirlpools.

So, hey! Don't be a wuss!

Be brave enough to go gladly into the inner as well as the outer spaces. You will be exhilarated, confounded, afraid [of the perceived unknown], enlightened, and amused. You will re-meet many old friends from eons past.

Enjoy the enlightenment and contacts that meditation will bring to you, for you do go into very real worlds. You meet with very real entities. You receive very real messages, and very real benefits from practicing meditation.

Real things come in real packages whether you can see and touch them or not. At this present time, the seekers will become more and more drawn into these intergalactic and inner realms and will meet more frequently the friends from the ancient eons.

It is a time of bringing into public awareness the messages of hope that have been well hidden or misinterpreted down through the Ages, and it is time to lift the lid off the box labelled "NO HOPE" and allow the negative beliefs within to disperse, then transmute into the light.

It is time for the Galactic Emissaries to contact the sensitive ones in your midst and begin to remove the collective memory blocks of mankind, to clear and strengthen the memory banks that have long remained dormant in most of the global citizens.

It is time for a grand resurgence of mankind's Spiritual aspects, and the thrumming of the vibrational energy within each and every Soul to beat as one heart, to love as one Soul, to become aware of HOME, and all that the name implies.

Can you feel the excitement building? Can you? Can you sense the magical, uplifting energy that is bubbling somewhere beneath the surface?

Maybe you do not know what surface and where this bubbling is coming from, but you know it is there. It is like a choir of angels tuning up before it bursts into radiant song. It is like the fanfare of Gabriel's Horn as it blasts through the walls of ignorance and despair. It is like the soft chortle of a songbird that is clearing its throat before it bursts into the most magnificent song that will ring out over the hilltops.

Oh, what excitement! Oh, what joy and happiness, and what a profound sense of love and emotion that comes overwhelmingly to the fore.

Please do not let your controlling thoughts take away your opportunity to connect with this magical upbeat. Go outside and sit beneath a tree, feel the pulse of the earth, take your mind away from thoughts of any environmental degradation that may or may not be present, feel the true beat that comes – "whoomp", "whoomp", "whoomp" – into your heart.

It is there, and it is able to be heard by you, and you, and you.

It is imperative that you believe that this is real. It is imperative for you to believe that this is not idle talk of an ancient old angel called Samuel. Cannot you feel the emotion rising within you? Cannot you feel the tears beginning to form within your eyes? Cannot you feel your heart constrict just that little bit, when you think of your true HOME?

Oh, beautiful readers, cannot you open up your heart even more to HOME, the HOME that you hold the key for, the golden key that opens the doors to your heart? Dearest, dearest readers, I am an emotional old angel, and I am full and bursting with happiness and love, with all emotions activated right now, and even I feel this joyful vibrational impulse or beat deep within you. Please sit quietly and listen for yourself. It is there; it is there.

Let us say at this point, your axis is shifting, whether you know it or not.

Samuel, do you mean a personal axis or the world axis?

The axis within each and every person, each and every living thing. Become an aware and balanced Soul. Become one who can remain steadily focused on the issues that affect this need for balance. You cannot remain in a neutral position. It is now your choice to connect in, or not, with this rising Universal heartbeat. It is your choice; it is your choice.

I am Samuel. You know me as Samuel the Prophet, and I bid each and every one a very insightful day.

Well, that was the most amazing book dictation session I have had for some time. Towards the end of the chapter, the energy, the intent, and the emotion continued to increase and increase in strength.

In the last third of the writing, I felt as though the heartbeat of this rising energy Samuel was talking about was being pounded into the words as I wrote them down. Pounded in, pounded in, and pounded in.

My hand was being pushed and pushed across the page. The people who will get to see the original handwritten manuscript will know exactly what was happening when they see the state of the handwriting.

I was getting the full sense of the 'rising heartbeat' and it made me feel so emotional. I was getting teary eyed and choked up with emotion. There was such a strong longing for HOME, with an intense connection of every fibre of me, to this uprising vibration.

I do realise that I feel only the tiniest, tiniest drop of Samuel's energy, yet it was enough to rock my world. Just think for a moment what immense strength and presence the full core of Samuel would emit.

Just think of the strength of presence any of us would have if we dared to open the conscious control panel and let the true 'us' out into the open. I don't know all the questions, let alone the answers to them, but after a book dictation such as this one just finished, the world does seem to be a better and more uplifting place.

The way does seem possible, for mankind to reach the heights of what we are all striving towards. It was, in all aspects, a magical morning's contact with my very good friend, Samuel the Prophet.

My final comment on today's session:

WOW!

11

SEMANTICS AND SURVIVAL

8 a.m. *Good morning, Samuel.*
Good day to you, dearest daughter.
You seem to be coming from a long, long way away.

No, it is only how you perceive the contact to be so this morning. I am always close, as close as your heartbeat. Now, this will be a good subject to speak more fully about.

It has been already mentioned, albeit briefly, but every aspect of your spiritual self can be spoken about on different levels and with different intensities. The closeness of your Spiritual Guides and Helpers is not measured in the length of distance as you know how to measure it with rulers and tapes and weird measuring devices. The closeness we speak of is the non-distance between heartbeats and the intensity of what you feel between these heartbeats.

Your comment about sensing me from a long way away is inaccurate because of the fact that you spoke of the measurement in physical measures, and not in the truthful concepts of vibrational movements. This is a common occurrence when people try and explain their spiritual 'closeness to Spirit'.

Of course, this is not a big deal, and indeed, most people would understand what is being meant, but it truly is a closeness of vibrational intensities more so than an Angel or Spirit entity of some type flapping its wings in a hurried journeying between the worlds of spirit and physical vibrational intensities.

We do not sit around on a cloud waiting for someone to ask us a question and then jump up from the cloud and fly or zoom in quickly to the nearest landing spot at the vicinity of the question-asking one. We are there already. It is our focus that locks onto where the question originated from. It is all a question of focal intensities and destinations.

As you feel my energy, and feel it to be either far or near, you are talking about the strengths of our vibrational energy contacts, and from what you feel from your end.

You live in a world, a universe of dancing, roiling, and vibrating energy, and we are all in this world 'soup' together – and it is not the huge physical movements within this soup that occur but the energy focus or fragment of a focal intensity, which instantaneously travels from one perceived point to another. If it was all a physical movement that occurred over any distance, there would be many sore and bruised heads. There would be clashes and bashes, bruises and bumps.

Yet you know that this scuffling and colliding is not happening, because even when you focus into new and different realities, you do so without the forceful slamming against someone else's focus that is also intent on travelling the inner pathways.

So, just be aware to not take everything you read in your spiritual literature and descriptions in a rigidly literal manner. You do need to realise that sometimes it can be very difficult to put down in mere words the explanations and descriptive insights, issues, and spiritual matters that are being explained to others.

The language known to the writer is put into everyday words and usages that others hopefully can understand, and this may mean using analogies of physical things that explain non-physical things. This is done deliberately so that the seeker who is just beginning the search for spiritual knowledge and answers has a framework of reference that brings in the physical aspects of known surroundings.

Thus, from the start, the sometimes overwhelming, scary, and maybe frightening spiritual experiences and lessons are grounded in something more familiar, and by this very physicalness, more comforting and non-threatening.

If we, as spiritual teachers, spoke to you wholly on a spiritual manner, you would think we were from some alien planet, one with a different language from the one you know and use. Teachers and Helpers will use whatever tools are needed to get the desired message across.

So, even though the idea of distance is incorrect, and it is, it will be used in a communicative way. Maybe you feel that I am picking at straws here, discussing something that does not seem to be so very important in the great scheme of things. You would be correct. But it is important for you at least to know that we are close, and we are within your heartbeat, even if you do describe the distance between you and one such as me as a long way away. Once you know of this closeness, you can describe it in whatever way you are able to.

Right, put that semantic squabble aside for the moment. The issue at stake here is not whose semantics are the correct ones. Rather, the issue is another word that begins with the letter 'S', and that word is 'survival'.

Yes, we speak of the survival of humanity as the next evolutionary step in being activated. To know fully what is happening about you, what is possible for you to do, and what you can expect to happen is more important than different word usages.

The more you understand that there is massive change looming, the more each and every person needs to prepare to meet all challenges that come along with all the twists and foibles of this vibrational change.

I may wander from the point at times, but even these side journeys with words have their validity. Many and varied are the techniques of teaching that have been utilised throughout the Ages and will continue to be used. Just as a driver or a passenger in the same automobile travelling to a certain destination will look out the car windows at the passing scenery, they will see different scenic views, each view seen from their own perspective, and through their own personal interpretive aspects.

Yet the journey continues until they reach the end. Both the passenger and the driver would probably give the same, yet obliquely different versions of what, in essence, is the same journey.

"Variety is the spice of life."

Have you heard this old adage?

It has been around in different forms for many, many heartbeats, but it remains a little nugget of truth and so it will survive all the retelling. The teachings, the different manners of style, the various teachers, all come together on the magical journey towards HOME. The viewpoints [as with the driver and the passenger] may be different, but the journey is the same.

I cannot reiterate this enough, the destination is the same and the bumps and faltering along the road will be dealt with by each person in their own way, but the journeying has the same intent.

Therefore, dearest readers, do not be narrowminded when it comes to listening to spiritual advice. Do not put your faith totally and exclusively into the one set of words, unless your gut instinct tells you strongly to do so.

Even a madman may spout forth a pearl of wisdom, a pearl of truth that comes tumbling out from amongst the incoherent thoughts expressed. The whole world around you is a wonderful teacher. Please do not ignore these teachings that are so freely and lovingly given. They are all around you. Do not limit yourself and concentrate on one thing only. Your journey path has reached a critical stage, and you will need all the helpful advice, love, and reassurance you can receive.

You have all heard of Angels, and of Spirit Guides. Well, I say this. Believe in them, and trust in them. But always check with your intuition and double-check again with your intuition, then see what your emotional beliefs hold about them, and then of course, trust the advice personally and intuitively given.

Accept the love, the insights, the information so freely and unconditionally given by the God of You. Believe in your own God light that burns brightly within you. It is there and burning brightly for all to see. The Cosmic Play is ready, and all the scenery is in place, and all the preparations have been made. The audience is ready and watching in anticipation of the most wonderful display of Light. They await the acting out of the play called "Life and Light", acted by a cast of multitudes.

Is this the "Divine Comedy"? Or is this the "Divine Aspects of Love"? I choose the latter as the more correct wordage for this drama's title. Which title would you choose? Or do you have another name in mind?

Hmm … Hmm?

Let us briefly say this. It does not truly matter what words are being spouted from someone's mouth. It is the inner intent, and the inner actions that are manifested into physical actions, that are the true barometers of an individual person's spiritual awareness. So, look at what people do and if you have to judge them in any way, then judge them by their actions.

You may have seen many glib people promising to do this or that, yet none of these promises are kept. Look for the quietly spoken person who goes around doing good deeds and know this person for the more spiritual person they are.

An easy and, indeed, classic example of this can be seen in the political arena. Do you vote for the aspiring politician who promises to get you massive tax cuts if elected, which you know will be a difficult or impossible promise to make good on, or do you vote for the more practical person who promises to get you the 10-20% tax cut that you know this candidate can probably achieve?

Now look very closely at your personal talk. Are you doing what you are telling everyone you are going to do, and are you giving yourself an honest assessment of your capabilities, or are you dishonestly fooling yourself?

Listen to what people say and include me amongst them. Make an intuitive decision on whether the speaker or writer is honestly practicing what he or she is preaching. Is it better to trust the teacher who has had personal experience, who has successfully dealt with all life situations, traumas, and life-threatening issues, or to trust the smooth teacher who has only theoretical knowledge and has no personal experience with the subject matter?

I usually opt for the teacher who has been personally involved and dealt with all contingencies; yet, at the same time, I acknowledge that all teachers have valid teachings as long as they are teaching for the right reasons.

12

DON'T HOLD YOUR BREATH

This is a shorter chapter to close out this book, with this set of semantics, thoughts expressed, and ideas freely offered.

Do you hold your breath when you are unsure of what to do or when you suddenly find yourself in a situation you are either afraid of or are unsure of? How long do you hold your breath? It cannot be for too long, otherwise your physical self will object strongly.

As mankind, *en masse*, stumbles along dealing in various ways with the rising universal vibrational energy, imagine mankind, again *en masse*, holding its collective breath while it waits for the next action or decisive moment. This breath is about to be released, and the breathing will then be able to continue in a more life-giving rhythm.

The Universe breathes in and then breathes out; everything in existence has this rhythmic movement on both interstellar and the proverbial 'grain of sand' scale. This movement cannot be stopped by you holding your breath [even if you realise that this is an analogy of you pausing between making decisions!]

Dear readers, there is no rest for you from this moving change. You are all in desperate need of more balance, and more steadying influences around you, so that you have a stable base from which to make balanced and informed decisions for your journeying through the maze of information and misinformation that you are constantly being bombarded with. You have the true power of discernment ready within you, just waiting to be invited out into the active arena and allowed to go to work joyfully on your behalf.

You are a personal powerhouse in a petite package. Do not feel that you are not in a position to make a huge and positive difference to everything that is happening on your beautiful planet. You, each and every one of you, is more powerful and Godlier than you realise. I know this, other Angels know this, and so it is our hopes and expectations that you also will remember that this is so.

Do not be just a mere mortal. Dare to become a majestic mortal, one who can jump mountains, one who is unafraid and confident in the past, present, and future of all times, one who knows they are an essential part of the Godly Whole!

Dare to be majestic!

I dare you to be thusly so!

And the swirling, looping signature of Samuel flowed across the page – and that was that; this book dictation now finished. I have already been told that the next book will be about what happens behind the scenes from the angelic side of things, from how Helpers work within guidelines, to why they work with specific people and situations, and generally how they go about their work.

Naturally, the title will be 'Behind The Scenes'.

About the Author

Helen Porteous had an upbringing in the magical Australian bush, and this fortunate lifestyle taught her a deep love of the natural worlds.

She was a prolific reader from a young age, with adventure, fantasy, and metaphysical stories amongst her favourites.

After a health crisis, she started meditation on a regular basis, and this triggered a new and deeper level of clairvoyance. This eventually led to the visitation of Mary, Samuel, and other Spirit entities, with incredible and ongoing friendships being formed.